HACKING
STUDENT
MOTIVATION

HACKING
STUDENT
MOTIVATION

5 Assessment Strategies That Boost Learning Progression & Build Student Confidence

HACK
Learning
SERIES

TYLER RABLIN

Hacking Student Motivation
© 2024 by Times 10 Publications
Highland Heights, OH 44143 USA
Website: 10publications.com

Cover and Interior Design by Michelle M. White
Editing by Tarah Threadgill
Copyediting by Jennifer Jas
Project Management by Regina Bell

Paperback ISBN: 978-1-956512-47-2
eBook ISBN: 978-1-956512-49-6
Hardcover ISBN: 978-1-956512-48-9

Library of Congress Cataloging-in-Publication Data is available for this title.

First Printing: February 2024

To my students, the reason I always want to be better.
This is for you.

To my colleagues and principals who encouraged me,
picked me up when I needed it,
and were there to talk about new ideas in education.
This is for you.

To my mom, the definition of strength and hope,
who battled cancer the entire time I was working on this book.
This is for you.

To my dad, who taught me what it means to be thoughtful
in our interactions with other people,
which is really the foundation of this book.
This is for you.

To my family and friends who are there for me
through the highs and lows of teaching and life.
This is for you.

Finally, to my wife, MaryBeth, who inspires me with her teaching and
has been my biggest source of encouragement through this process.
You have given me the love I needed when things got tough.
This is for you.

TABLE OF CONTENTS

INTRODUCTION

Find a Reason to Move

If I set a bear loose in your campsite, you would probably jump up and hopefully even run away. Now, before you start wondering why this is the opening line to a book about education, I need you to bear with me for a moment (yes, pun intended). Why would you suddenly move? Some of you might think, "Well, I moved because I enjoy my life and would like it to carry on past this bear's next meal." Others might answer, "It was purely out of fear, and instinct took over." Still more might say, "I was just trying to be faster than my slowest friend." Essentially, the goal was simply to avoid pain and punishment. To survive.

Those answers all miss a simple truth: we had a reason to move. Had I never brought that bear into the campground, everyone would have continued lounging around the campfire with their favorite beverage in hand and no plans of moving for quite a while. There would have been no movement, save for the trips to the cooler for a refill or the snack table for some chips. Everyone would have been content with the lack of movement. It's not a willful act of disobedience; rather, it's the natural way our brains work. When we don't see a reason to move or act, it frankly feels weird if we do. (Note: As someone who loves the outdoors, I have to mention that it's a terrible idea to run from a bear in an actual bear encounter.)

Here is the phrase I think about all the time in my teaching life: *We move when we have a reason to.* And when we have no reason to move, we are content with the lack of movement and may even *desire* the lack of movement.

On top of this, not all reasons to move are equal. A bear running into my campsite? Pretty good motivation to move. If that didn't get me moving, I would either have the nerve of Crocodile Dundee or a complete disregard for my own well-being. However, if a friend stood up around the campfire and invited me to go for a jog on a trail, that might also be a reason to move. I would probably recognize that the jog would improve my health, but the motivation may not be powerful enough to get me out of the camping chair and away from the fire. Reasons to move are highly individualized. For example, while I may not be thrilled to go on a jog when I could roast marshmallows instead, you may relish the trail run.

Student motivation in school is one of the most complicated scenarios we encounter every day with anywhere from tens of students at the primary level to hundreds of students at the secondary level. Each one of those students reacts differently to different reasons to move. As we begin this book, I don't want to downplay the reality that helping students tap into their motivation is one of the most complex, difficult elements we face in the classroom. The problem is that tapping into student motivation, building their confidence, and empowering them are part of our most important jobs as educators. So, one of our most difficult roles in the classroom is also one of the most crucial aspects of our jobs.

The 2019–2020 school year was incredibly difficult, and every educator who went through the rapid shift to remote learning deserves a gold medal, a gigantic raise (in addition to the pay raise we all deserve as it is), and a tropical vacation where no one can email us. Yet as I write this in the summer of 2023, we just finished up what has arguably been one of the most difficult years for teachers that I can remember.

What surprised most people is that the year we returned to the classroom full-time, for many, ended up being even more difficult than the last. Something had shifted. I heard many educators refer to it as a new pandemic: one of missing work and unmotivated students. Countless reasons exist for why this shift occurred, and I want to emphasize that all of them are valid and real. Collectively, we were dealing with the aftermath of a pandemic and the stress therein, health issues or the loss of a loved one, and societal shifts in terms of the rules that previously determined how we lived. Students weren't immune to any of these issues, either.

While talking about issues and grappling with our new way of life are vital on a global scale, the scope of this book is more focused. If these past few years have taught me anything, it's to look for the spaces where I can make a positive difference; for many of us educators, we have that opportunity every day in our classrooms with our students.

The impact of the major changes in society in the past few years seems to manifest as an apparent lack of motivation in our students. I know that for many of us, it felt like pulling teeth to convince students to engage in learning like we were accustomed to in the past. Add to that a rapidly changing attention economy, where apps and websites are intentionally designed to keep us on them for longer stretches of time. As such, students seem to be more invested in their phones than ever before, and teaching, at times, feels like shouting into a void.

It's frustrating, and I don't want to overlook this reality. I had days when I struggled to feel like I was anywhere near effective. Here's the part that's difficult to swallow, though. It will continue to be frustrating so long as we try the same tactics to motivate students. That isn't to say what we did previously was wrong, but rather, what we did before the pandemic no longer works in the same ways.

I think about the game-based formative assessment tools I previously used to review material and check understanding in class. Do kids still enjoy them? Absolutely. We still have fun, but what's changed is that it seems like the glitz and glamour have worn off; the effects are not as long-lasting. What used to keep kids excited and motivated to engage in the work for a whole class period now seems ineffective, and they fade a few minutes after the game has ended. Why? Probably many reasons, but one that we can't overlook is that there are more engaging games available to students in the palms of their hands these days than I can offer them in a school context.

Is this a bad situation? Again, it's frustrating in the moment, but think about what it points out. If glitz and glamour were the only values the student saw in the learning process, what does that tell us about how learning happens in the classroom? What does it tell us about student motivation? If we want students to truly engage in their learning, we must look past surface-level motivation, which can be fun in the moment, and search for ways to push them toward a deeper, meaningful, and more sustained motivation founded on long-term growth, confidence, and success. We must tap into the elements of intrinsic motivation that Daniel Pink summarized in his book *Drive* as autonomy, purpose, and mastery.

While the technological shift drastically changed a myriad of things, a bigger and more important shift happened over the past few years. Think about the primary way students were encouraged to engage in school. I bet if you and I were talking about this in person, we could count to three and say the same word at the same time: grades.

What was (arguably) supposed to measure progress toward the goal of learning ended up completely eclipsing the initial goal and the culture of school—both within our buildings and outside of them. Thus, we often take actual learning out of the equation and instead value only the letter grades mailed home in each report card. Especially at the secondary level, kids generally aren't as concerned as much with learning as they are with getting good grades. This message is reinforced over and over by guardians, teachers, guidance counselors, and college applications.

Then came the pandemic. In the rapid shift to remote learning and trying to restructure the understanding that students have about what school is and how learning happens, many students saw for the first time what they'd been trying to avoid their entire school career: an F. Though grading was relaxed a bit at first, eventually, the ratchets tightened down and schools saw a wave of failure rates that sent administrators and teachers reeling. In the planning and scrambling to try to get students back on track and get credit recovery systems in place, the education system overlooked one critical component.

Many students lost their reason to move.

The motivator of that high grade point average (GPA) that dangled in front of students for so long was suddenly snatched away. I saw straight-A students get their first F during remote learning and proceed to fail class after class the following year. A student I'd had prior to the pandemic, a wonderful student, came back to check in with me about halfway through the year following remote learning, and when I asked how they were doing in classes, they became sheepish. A quick grade check almost jolted me out of my chair. They had gone from almost straight As their ninth grade year to almost straight Fs by their junior year. When I asked what had happened, they confirmed my fears. They told me that they always thought they were a good student, but when they failed a class during remote learning, they felt like they just weren't a good student anymore and that their goals of going to college and getting a good grade point average had gone out the window.

Many other students share that story. I'm sure if you went in and checked the grades of many former students from before the pandemic, you would see similar examples. This should raise red flags everywhere. We preach grit and resilience like they are qualities a student can pull on like a T-shirt, and suddenly, they are willing to push through the tough times. It doesn't work like that, and that thinking blames the student for failure when we really should be thinking about how the education system has failed.

When grades became the goal, we set up our students and ourselves for failure. We focused on the quickest and easiest way to motivate students, and then we centered our entire educational approach on a flawed perspective.

However, there is hope for a better way. In recent years, a growing push has emerged to de-emphasize traditional grades and center classroom culture back on learning, whether it's through standards-based learning, mastery-based learning, gradelessness, or ungrading. Teachers all over are pushing back on the idea that grades are the only worthwhile goal.

That's what this book is intended to do but with a slightly different slant. Yes, focusing on learning through a more meaningful way to assess students is a topic I'm incredibly passionate about, but it's not what I'm most passionate about. What I'm most passionate about is helping to create students who are motivated to move the needle of their learning for meaningful reasons, empowered to make a difference in the world around them, and confident enough in themselves to try without a grade or other measure hanging over their heads. These are the students we need for the future of our world.

While that idea is grandiose, this book is about how we can make changes in the way we assess students through both small and larger shifts within our classrooms. This book is about how we can use assessment to show students their competence and their next steps, not just have them dwell on their mistakes. It's about how we can help students who don't feel like school is for them see early success that can create lasting impacts on how they perceive their capabilities. It's about recognizing that a change has occurred and that it doesn't have to be a bad change. Rather, this change has highlighted realities left covered for too long. Kids have never been truly and meaningfully motivated by grades. It's a surface-level performance we all play in within our school walls. Yet, we've treated grades as if they are an unshakable truth about how motivation works, and along the way, we ignored the students who never felt successful or motivated by this definition of success.

Throughout my journey as an educator, I, too, often thought "cared about grades" meant the same as "cared about learning" and too often blamed students when they weren't motivated by the artificial definition of success that I dangled in front of them. This book is not my success story. I will never be able to write that book because this isn't a process that ever comes to an ending point. There is no finish line, and that's what makes it exciting to pursue a more equitable, more empowering, and more meaningful method of motivating students in my classroom.

This book is a collection of the methods I've tried, failures I've encountered, and stories of the incredible kids I got to work with along the way. This book carries the best I have to offer for anyone in a situation like mine who wants to do better inside the constraints of the existing educational system.

To anyone who feels that way, no matter where you're at in your journey with assessment, here's your reminder: it's possible, and it is so completely worth it. When you see that a change in your approach to assessment results in a student *moving* and not giving up and instead pushing themself even more, it's worth it. When you see a student who would have been content with a decent grade go above and beyond to put in discretionary energy because they have developed a sense of confidence that allows them to take risks in their learning, it's worth it. No matter what, the pursuit of trying to do better by kids is worth it.

With that, let's move.

HACK 1

DESIGN AN INFORMATIVE GRADE BOOK

Communicate Progress and Growth Rather than Completion and Grades

I have a love-hate relationship with grades because I like seeing that I have all A's, but at the same time, even when you have a perfect 4.0, you are not happy . . .
I don't think teachers see how that affects a student's mental health.

— ANONYMOUS STUDENT ON A GRADING SURVEY

THE PROBLEM:
TRADITIONAL GRADES DON'T PROMOTE MEANINGFUL ENGAGEMENT

I still remember the exact moment I realized my grade book was absolutely meaningless. It was 2013, and I was finishing up the year at McLoughlin High School in Milton-Freewater, Oregon. This was before anyone trusted an online grade book enough for us to submit our final grades digitally. As such, I was walking down the hallway to the office with my grade book in hand, and as I flipped through the pages, I realized I knew nothing more about my students' learning than I would have known without them.

For context before we really dive in, see Image 1.1 for an idea of what my grade book looked like as I carried it down the hallway.

	QUIZ 1	UNIT NOTES	WORK-SHEET	QUIZ 2	REVIEW	UNIT TEST	FINAL GRADE
STUDENT A	7	10	5	8	10	23	84%
STUDENT B	4	5	0	3	10	27	65%
STUDENT C	8	10	5	8	10	19	80%

Image 1.1: Sample contents in my old grade book.

I taught mostly eleventh grade students at the time, and I pictured handing my grade book to their twelfth grade teacher and saying, "I want you to have this so that you know what your incoming students need to focus on." They would laugh, I would laugh, and then we would continue doing the same lessons without knowing why year after year.

That moment in the hallway, inside a hundred-year-old brick building, standing on an old carpet covered with stains, I made a decision. I decided I didn't want to be like that building, stuck in an antiquated system. I wanted to change, to renovate the way I assessed students, and to do it better. I dropped off the grade book, went back to my classroom, and started to figure out how to do it better.

I didn't have a classroom built for learning; I had a vending machine for grades—put an assignment in, get a grade out.

To start with, I had to pinpoint the problems before trying to solve them. I pulled up the backup copy of my grade book and stared at it for a long time, returning again and again to one very simple idea: the point of any form of academic records is to clearly communicate where a student is in their learning. The root of the problem is that my grade book wasn't communicating what I wanted it to. It fell short.

My epiphany about the meaninglessness of my grade book was that it focused on tasks, not learning. Ask any student what they need to do to improve their grade, and almost all of them will talk about the tasks and assignments they need to complete. Do students still need to complete certain tasks to prove evidence of learning? Yes, but that's not what I wanted students to solely focus on. The tasks, like quizzes and projects, were meant to be vehicles, the means to an end, and yet because of the way my grade book was set up, the tasks were the priority, the most prominent piece of the grade book connected to the final grade.

Essentially, I didn't have a classroom built for learning; I had a vending machine for grades—put an assignment in, get a grade out. I was creating grade-hungry monsters in my classroom who didn't even seem to recognize that learning was involved in any part of that process, and it showed. Each task was an island of performance, and students were skipping from each one, doing a task and moving on to the next seemingly disconnected task. Rarely did I get to talk about learning. Instead, I had conversations about points: "How do I get my grade up?" "How many points is this assignment worth?" I had to find a way to shift that dialogue, that mindset, so that we focused on learning. My challenge: How do I develop a grade book that centers the learning, not the tasks meant to support it?

Now, did these assignments provide me with *some* data? Absolutely. If a student struggled on a quiz, I knew to check in with that student. If a student didn't complete the notes, I knew we needed to have a conversation. If the whole class failed a test, I knew I had some reteaching to do.

However, there were two problems with this structure. First, I was still focused on tasks. Often, the way I responded to a student who failed a test was to have them retake the test. Missing notes? Come in and see me during an intervention time to get the notes.

Second, and most important, the data I had wasn't useful because it was overly cumbersome in identifying trends and patterns. For example, if the unit test covered multiple topics, how was I supposed to know which topic specifically needed my attention and more class time? If I were going to pull out a small group for an intervention, how was I supposed to quickly identify which students needed support in which topics if I were taking all that information and combining it into a single score for "test" in the grade book?

I had a lot of data but not a lot of information. By this, I mean that I had a lot of numbers and nowhere to go with them. One of the most valuable efforts we can make for our students is to help them see their success and growth. My grade book didn't show that.

My goal was to find a way to organize that information so it was quick and easy to understand what needed to happen and for whom.

It was like some weird game of Twister, where each skill was awkwardly intertwined with all the other skills in that unit. I wanted students to be able to look at the record of their learning and easily be able to tell me where they were growing and where they were stuck without having to untwist their grading data to do it. Often, because we covered multiple standards in a unit, one assignment in the grade book would be about one skill, and then the next assignment would be about a different skill. As a result, when you looked through the grade book, it wasn't a record of growth about a specific skill but rather a smattering of concepts that were stepping over each other. I needed to make it quick and easy to identify trends in their learning.

THE HACK:
DESIGN AN INFORMATIVE GRADE BOOK

Standards-based grading in and of itself is not revolutionary. It does not guarantee that assessment will become meaningful in your classroom, that your classroom will be a more equitable place, and that your students will become highly motivated learners.

Standards-based grading does one simple and powerful job: it opens doors to the type of classroom where students understand how to be active, motivated participants in their learning process. Once those doors are open, however, the work remains to be done in terms of pedagogical approaches to the way we design learning and assessments. A standards-based approach to assessment, when paired with an increase in student ownership in the learning process, was the doorway to a richer learning environment in my classroom.

> *Instead of asking, "What do I want my students to do?" it forced me to start thinking, "What do I want my students to know?"*

Standards-based grading is a natural starting point, and it's an important one because it forces a shift in the instruction and assessment in the classroom to focus on specific standards and goals. For me, it helped me change where I start planning. Instead of asking, "What do I want my students to do?" it forced me to start thinking, "What do I want my students to know?" When we start with that question, we create more freedom, both in our teaching and in how students can experience their learning. When I start by creating what I want students to *do*, I'm narrowing the room for creativity, choice, and individuality, and it often means I began by building an assessment. When I shifted to focus on the learning first, I realized that I had opportunities for students to exert some control over how they learned the content and how they demonstrated their learning.

This autonomy for students, the ability to have some control over an experience, is a huge element of motivation. For example, when I was a kid, one of my jobs was to mow the lawn. I was told to do it. I hated it, absolutely hated it. It was like pulling teeth to get me to do it. As an adult with my own house and lawn, now I find myself in full-blown dad-mode, getting excited to get out and work in the yard. Did the task change? Did the person involved change? No, it is still me mowing the lawn. The difference? I am in control of it, and as a result, I take more pride in it. It is meaningful to me because I can choose if, when, and how to do it.

This is just one of the doors that can be opened by standards-based assessment and learning: the ability to increase the autonomy that students experience and to create an avenue for students to truly see their growth. When I was focused on isolated tasks in my grade book, growth was difficult to spot. Yes, there was an increase in quiz scores, but what did that mean about the learning? Additionally, growth in a quiz connects to an artificial goal. That quiz is arbitrary, but when the growth is visible in terms of the learning the student is engaged in, the knowledge is building inside their brain. That ability to see growth is a huge factor in motivation. When we see we're growing, we believe we have the capacity to be successful in later attempts, and when we believe that, we have a solid foundation for motivation to grow.

Seeing self-growth communicates to students that no matter where they start, they have the potential to be successful. Here's an example to illustrate this: In a traditional grade book, where the final grade is a simple average of the attempts over time, a student who scores low on the first attempt will always have a lower average score than someone who came in with a better understanding of the concept. Even if those two students end up performing at equal levels in later attempts to demonstrate their learning, if we average scores over time, like my grade book did at the beginning of my career, we are telling students, "Where you come from will dictate how far you can go." Obviously, we would never say that outright to a student, but grading is a form of communication, and if we are holding students accountable for their early attempts at learning without the opportunity for better subsequent attempts, that's the message we are communicating.

These two elements of motivation, autonomy and visible growth, come from a re-prioritization of the grade book. For me, this meant that my headers in my grade book were no longer labeled as tasks, but rather, those headers were the learning students engaged in. Underneath that was a record of how they performed on those skills over time. This allowed me to both see the growth and to value it when it came time to determine a final score for each skill. See Image 1.2.

SKILL			
	Attempt 1	Attempt 2	Attempt 3	Current
STUDENT A				
STUDENT B				
STUDENT C				

Image 1.2: My current learning-focused grade book.

Your grade book redesign can look countless ways, but they all start with a simple question: "How does my grade book communicate that the most important goal in the classroom is learning and growth?" It was this question that helped me redesign my grade book so that it built motivation instead of hindered it.

While that question is complex and may require major changes, which are detailed step-by-step in the full implementation section later, simply asking that question turned out to be the hack I didn't realize my whole classroom needed.

WHAT YOU CAN DO TOMORROW

Redesigning your entire grade book can seem daunting at first. However, you can practice prioritizing learning in the assessment process in a few ways without a full overhaul of the grade book.

▶ **Talk to or survey your students.** Sometimes, the hardest part of this journey to make assessment more powerful in our classrooms is identifying a powerful reason for change. At the beginning of every year, I ask my students, in an anonymous survey, three simple questions:

1. Do grades help you learn?
2. How do grades make you feel?
3. Why do teachers use grades?

The student responses are often painful to hear, but it's those responses that help pinpoint my reason for doing this work, both within my classroom and with other schools. Here are some of the comments my students wrote on this year's survey.

1. **Do grades help you learn?**

   - "Yes and no because when I get a bad grade, I have no motivation to do it anymore or I feel dumb, but when I get a good decent grade, I strive for better."
   - "No not really. Grades are something that just either boosts your confidence or brings it wayyy down."
   - "Yes, because I feel pressured to do better."

2. **How do grades make you feel?**

   - "Dumb."
   - "Like I just need to pass to show I am learning."
   - "I honestly don't like grades. When you don't have good grades, people will think you're unintelligent, but you could be a gifted person and just morally

hate school and other systems ... for college to think that you're not smart because you have bad grades or messed up your grades just seems wrong to me."

- "Kind of anxious cause you never know if it'll go down or not."

3. **Why do teachers use grades?**

- "To show how many assignments you have finished."
- "To be honest idk."
- "To judge us."

This happens every year. Every time I get a new batch of students, I get a clear reminder of the ways grades can be weaponized in our schools, and here's the worst part: kids are absolutely aware of it.

So, if you need a reason to persevere when times get tough, listen to your kids. Give them space to voice how grading and assessment impact them, and I have no doubt you will find the push you are looking for.

▶ **Create or research assessment blueprints.** I'm a big fan of using assessment blueprints as a guide to take your existing assessments and think about what each question shows you about the student's learning. The concept behind them is incredibly simple yet powerful in its ability to shift our thinking around designing assessments and how we collect data. The idea behind an assessment blueprint is that you are categorizing the questions or parts of an assessment based on the standard, skill, or content each question asks students to demonstrate. See Image 1.3 for an example of an assessment blueprint.

QUESTION	STANDARD/ESSENTIAL LEARNING

Image 1.3: An assessment blueprint.

Assessment blueprints are that simple. They open the door to two important processes. First, as an audit for our assessment to make sure we are assessing what we've taught. I can't tell you how many times, early in my career, I caught myself assessing something we hadn't really covered in class. This step helps avoid that issue. Second, having a blueprint makes it easier to figure out how to record scores for individual standards, skills, and content. It begins the process of breaking down the all-encompassing cumulative score that doesn't hold much value in terms of future learning (unless the assessment only focuses on one standard, of course). It's a step in the right direction, and a very important one at that.

▶ **Keep records of one skill at a time.** If the idea of overhauling your entire grade book all at once is intimidating, try starting small. For an upcoming unit, select just one key skill that students will focus on, and practice collecting evidence of their learning by using a table to record their attempts and progress. This will help you test the waters. Whenever students demonstrate their use of the one key skill, add the data to your table. When you're about halfway through, take a minute to look at the sheet and think about the type of information it gives you and what you can do with it. Can you find a student who's shown growth that you can celebrate? Could you pull together a few students for a reteaching moment? Can you see a student who's not making progress and who could use a pep talk or a check-in? The value in this step doesn't lie in simply gathering the data but in pausing to think about what you and your students could do with that data.

▶ **Create a grade book for your next unit.** Redesigning your grade book and keeping it transparent for students is the next crucial step in unlocking standards-based grading as the vehicle for building student motivation. However, this doesn't mean it's a complete overhaul of your entire grade book overnight. I'm a person who often jumps in with both feet and figures it out as I go, but in working with many educators to redesign their grade books, I've realized that many teachers just want to test it out. Maybe it would work best for you to start with just one standard that you track over a single unit. Even small steps like this allow you to begin building the practices that tap into motivation.

What could this look like? Try starting with a spreadsheet. Have sections labeled with the specific learning outcomes for the unit and then multiple columns under each section for different attempts to demonstrate that learning. Remember, the point isn't what it looks like. The point is how it functions in building student motivation by providing them with clear evidence of their learning. How can you create a method of recordkeeping that is organized by learning, creates space for multiple attempts, and values growth? Remind yourself and your students that success doesn't look any one specific way. The goal is a more equitable, accurate, and student-oriented way of documenting learning that provides transparency for students so they can become active participants in the assessment process.

A BLUEPRINT FOR FULL IMPLEMENTATION

STEP 1   STEP 2   STEP 3   STEP 4   STEP 5

Analyze your standards and identify your priorities.

It's impossible to adequately cover all the standards educators are supposed to get every student to learn. Sometimes, we just need to say that out loud because, as educators, we are notoriously bad at admitting we can't do it all. To start, sit down with a unit of study and ask yourself the following question: "What do kids *really* need to know?" I'm sure your pacing guide or curriculum scope and sequence says a lot about this, and I'm sure the person selling the curriculum to your school used the word "fidelity" a lot to try to strong-arm decision-makers into believing that everything is absolutely essential, but let's be real. Not everything we're expected to teach students is essential.

Many schools call the process "identifying your priority standards." Essentially, you're looking for standards that are most important, not just in your classroom but in classrooms of other content areas, in applications outside the world of academia, and in subsequent classes of the same content. Standards that are more important in those three areas should end up being a priority standard.

Examine your upcoming unit and identify the essential pieces of learning that students need to know. This depends on the length of your unit of study, but often, in a four-week unit of study, I identify two or three essential pieces of learning. This allows the time and space to provide students with multiple opportunities to demonstrate learning, receive feedback, engage in reteaching, and try again. If you don't limit the number of learning pieces you're trying, you may feel overwhelmed, and so will your students. Less is more, especially when depth and growth are the goals.

STEP 1 **STEP 2** **STEP 3** **STEP 4** **STEP 5**

Reorganize your recordkeeping.

While it's theoretically possible to simply use the online grade book to keep track of student data in a meaningful way, almost everyone I know who has been doing some form of standards-based grading for a while has their own method of keeping track of student data outside of the official online grade book. Yes, eventually, the information needs to be recorded in the official grade book (more on that in step 5 in this section), but I have found much more success in using a spreadsheet to track this data. I've been intentional with this recordkeeping in four major ways to ensure it gives me data I can use to help students build their motivation.

First, my headers switched from tasks (such as quizzes and tests) to skills (such as to use evidence in writing and analyze word choice). Initially, my grade book looked like the example in Image 1.4.

	TASK	TASK	TASK
STUDENT A			
STUDENT B			
STUDENT C			

Image 1.4: My initial task-focused grade book.

Each column was its own separate island of information, and it was hard for me to track growth and see trends. After making the switch, now my grade book looks like the example in Image 1.2 (which you saw earlier in this chapter).

SKILL			
	Attempt 1	Attempt 2	Attempt 3	Current
STUDENT A				
STUDENT B				
STUDENT C				

Image 1.2: My current learning-focused grade book.

You'll notice that the main header is organized by the skill, and this allows me to arrange the data in a much more useful way. This shift helped to set up the second way I rearranged my grade book, and that was to create space for multiple attempts at a skill. If you look underneath the main header in the previous table, the sub-headings identify different attempts at a skill. This allows me to see growth, and more importantly for the student and their motivation, it allows them to see their own growth. With this setup, I can quickly spot growth and say to a student, "Hey, look at how you were struggling early on, but now you are showing that you're starting to get it." That conversation alone is incredibly powerful in supporting student confidence and motivation.

Third, I shifted my system of records to a smaller and more consistent scoring scale. Yes, the traditional hundred-point scoring scale does have the potential to show growth, but that growth is hard to explain and understand. If I moved from a seventy-five to a seventy-six in a specific skill, I may not know what I learned to change the number. More importantly, I don't know what I need to do to get to a seventy-seven. This lack of clarity can often become a barrier to motivation because students don't know how to take ownership of their learning to get to that next level. As such, I shifted my scoring scale to be out of five points, making each step clearer and more tangible for students.

Finally, the last major element of the grade book redesign for me was to create a column for a cumulative score. I like to call this column the "current score" to communicate that it is always changing and it simply records where each student is at now. What this allowed me to do was to move away from simply averaging those scores over time because now I had a dedicated space to record, as accurately as possible, the level that best represents each student's understanding. This is a key to unlocking the door to student conferencing, which has been one of the biggest motivators in my classroom since I began implementing it.

STEP 1   STEP 2   STEP 3   STEP 4   STEP 5

Map your assessments to specific standards.

I used to lean heavily on traditional tests—you know the ones with multiple-choice questions and a few short response questions—when I began teaching. That's not to say they hold no value, but I know they didn't in the way I was using them. First, I couldn't explain what skill each question was connected to. Often, I just had a big unit test where the skills were jumbled in among the questions, spread out with no apparent rhyme or reason.

Then I stumbled across the idea of the assessment blueprint, which we looked at earlier in this chapter. Even before I switched to a standards-based system, this change ended up bringing more value to the ways that I could use the information from an assessment. Because I had mapped the assessment to standards, I could look at the scores and say, "Oh, a lot of students struggled with question three, so we need to spend more time going over this specific skill." I could also better use the data with students. I could say, "These four questions focused on this skill, and these four focused on this other skill. I want you to look at your results and decide which small group you need to join today for the practice."

When educators map the assessment questions to specific standards, and especially when we organize them in meaningful ways as a result, we can begin to put the data and information back into the hands of students so they can use them to guide their own learning.

STEP 1   STEP 2   STEP 3   **STEP 4**   STEP 5

Test it out on a small scale (and with a safety net).

Once you have your grade book redesigned and your assessments mapped to specific standards and skills, it's useful to test it out on a small scale before fully overhauling your whole grading system. What worked for me was to focus on one skill for the unit that I wanted to track and to practice this new approach to recordkeeping. This gave me some wiggle room to try out different approaches as I asked myself, "How can I record this information in the clearest way possible?"

For me, this ended up being on a spreadsheet, but it can simply be a piece of paper you jot notes on with columns for different attempts. Maybe you want to try it out with students recording their own scores over time on a worksheet or in a portfolio. Whatever you try, test different ideas and always look for how they impact students and their motivation.

I recommend testing it out on a small scale first. I made many mistakes in trying to jump in too quickly. Take small steps and constantly ask these questions. Is it equitable? Is it accurate? Is it transparent?

Equity, accuracy, and transparency—once you have a method that prioritizes those, you're on the right track. If that's a spreadsheet separate from your grade book, great. That's how I started. If students are recording this data on their own in a portfolio, also great. If you are a better grading software magician than me and have found a way to use your existing grade book to communicate all this in a way that is equitable, accurate, and transparent ... well, you'd better trademark something because that's the million-dollar idea.

STEP 1   STEP 2   STEP 3   STEP 4   STEP 5

Figure out how to make this approach work within your existing grading program.

One of the biggest barriers to building assessment systems that motivate students to learn is the typical online grading program. They are almost always designed to focus students on tasks, not learning. If we want to motivate students to focus on their learning, we must learn how to hack the grading program to make it work for us and our students.

Here are three methods I've used and the pros and cons of each.

- **Create categories based on each piece of essential learning.** Most grading programs have an option to do category weighting. In this option, you create a category for each piece of essential learning in the unit (e.g., for my ELA class, I might have a category called "Supporting Ideas with Evidence" and another called "Using Introductions in Writing").

Pro: Almost every grading software I've seen reports a score for each category. Usually, this focuses on tests, quizzes, and projects, but if we reframe to focus on learning, we can use the grading software to help report on individual learning objectives without having to do too much modifying on our own.

Con: Usually, the way this score is calculated is by averaging the scores from the entire term into a single score. As mentioned before, this method doesn't value growth and penalizes students for early mistakes. This means that to avoid that scenario, you might need to go in and exempt old assignments to keep them from pulling down the average for that category, which can be time-intensive (and that means I wouldn't want any teacher to add it to their plate).

▶ **Use the built-in standards features.** While most grade books aren't centered on standards, many developers are starting to catch on that a growing number of teachers want to focus on them. This means that many big-name grading programs (such as Skyward, PowerSchool, and Infinite Campus) and some learning management systems (such as Schoology and Canvas) do have a standards-based option built in.

Pro: Usually, with this method, you have options for how to calculate the scores of each standard, which grants the flexibility to prioritize more recent scores. In addition, reporting options are typically built in to communicate these scores with students and caregivers in an easy, user-friendly way.

Con: Most of the major grading programs don't make the standards-based options super user-friendly, especially if you are an individual teacher looking to try this out.

▶ **Use it only for what I need to communicate to caregivers and administrators.** This is the system I currently use. I have one category for "Standards" and one for "Assignments." My goal is simply to think about what key stakeholders outside the classroom need to know, and then I use the online grade book to communicate about those topics. Inside my classroom, my students and I operate on a different set of information that focuses on learning.

In my experience with families, they want to know a few things: (1) Are their students staying on top of their work, (2) Are they learning what they need to learn, and (3) How are they behaving in class? (The last one is a bonus, and I'm honestly super grateful to work in a community that cares so much about this.)

As such, I communicate the two categories (Standards and Assignments) separately in the online grade book. For the Assignments category, I simply record if it was done, missing, or completed late. This communicates whether the student is staying on top of their work, but here's the key: It's not factored into their actual grade. It is only for communication purposes.

The Standards category counts for almost the entirety of their grade. For this, I have one assignment per skill, and I update that score throughout the term. By communicating these two details, I can keep caregivers informed without creating an online grade book that focuses students on the wrong information.

Pro: Recording assignments simply as completed or missing allows me to input them into the online grade book in a timely fashion. The day an assignment is supposed to be turned in, I can immediately communicate whether it was finished. Before, I used to wait until all assignments were graded to input scores, at which point, it could be weeks before the parent (and sometimes even the student) knew they missed something.

Con: It takes a lot of communication. In my early attempts at this, I didn't explain the details well to students or caregivers, and I had a lot of questions about the marks students were receiving (or not receiving). At times, it caused tension. In addition, the other hurdle I've had to overcome is that when students see their work marked as either done or not done, it can encourage them to simply rush through their work to finish it. This takes retraining, and the best way I've found to do this is to identify early on which students rushed through things, talk with them privately about it, and ask them to re-attempt it. While it might take a little more effort up front, I've found that setting the bar high early goes a long way in helping students understand that just getting an assignment done is not the goal. Learning requires effort, and as such, they need to be putting in effort on their assignments. However, when students understand that if they put in effort, they have the space they need to make mistakes and grow from them, it creates an environment where motivation can grow.

While there are other ways to hack traditional grade books in a standards-based system, these are the three I have used and have seen be successful within other classrooms, too.

OVERCOMING PUSHBACK

If any aspect of the education world should win an award for the amount of pushback it receives, standards-based grading would probably be at the top of the podium with a medal. This often comes from a lack of understanding, but there are also valid concerns and critiques. Honestly, I've gone through my own periods of running into concerning areas of standards-based grading, but in the end, the value of helping students focus on the learning instead of just checking the boxes ends up outweighing the pushback. Here are common areas of pushback and their responses.

This is too much work! I won't lie. Initially, yes, it's more setup, but the best way I can explain this is through the analogy of food. Eating healthy can initially feel like a lot more work, especially if it's not a habit you're used to. Is it a lot easier to get fast food on the way home from work than it is to prepare a nutritious meal on your own? Yeah, absolutely. The problem is that the easy route doesn't hold as much value as the more difficult route. With my original grade book, it was simple, but it was also the equivalent of junk food. It was technically data, but it wasn't valuable as information. Did it take a lot of work to make the switch? Absolutely, but I want to help you avoid the dead ends I ran into along the way.

Just like how it gets easier to eat healthy once you've figured out food you like and how to meal plan, standards-based grading gets much, much easier with time. You'll start to develop evidence-gathering routines, learn how to help students develop their abilities to assess themselves around clear standards, and find out what you can cut to make the workload more manageable.

I always hear this pushback when I encourage people to pursue changes in their assessment practices because as a full-time teacher, I know that everyone is overworked. I promise you this, though. I wouldn't encourage people to pursue this if I didn't know (1) how transformative it can be to our classrooms and (2) that after the transition, it can end up saving you time in the long run.

It's just playing with numbers. Sadly, this misconception is often justified because I hear it when the rationale for the shift to standards-based grading is to increase graduation rates or decrease the number of Fs students receive in classes. If that's the case, then yes, it's just playing with numbers. However, the real reason is so much more important than that. Can the number of Fs decrease in a switch to standards-based grading because student grades are no longer driven by compliance? Absolutely. Can kids still receive Fs because they are held accountable for learning a standard? Also yes. The point is that if we make it a metric that is measured by failure rates or whatever else we want to put on our fancy data walls, then yes, it can seem like playing with numbers.

However, the key to responding to this is focusing on how it can impact teaching and learning. Measuring the effectiveness of assessment methods by talking about the number of specific grades makes no sense. The point of an assessment system isn't grades or grading. The point is to inform learning. When we focus on that, it's where we can really see the value in standards-based grading.

While all of this is important, it doesn't capture the true essence of why this matters. When you walk into a classroom that uses a standards-based approach to allow students the ability to pursue mastery, to learn from their mistakes, and to focus on learning, you can feel a palpable change in the atmosphere. You can feel the motivation coming from students because they can see their growth and feel confident because they have clarity of purpose and can take ownership of it.

The kids won't understand it. To be honest, many students don't understand regular grading, either, especially when we use random grade penalties like, "If you turn in a late assignment, you will lose 25 percent of your score unless you've submitted it on the second Tuesday of the new moon and provide me with the secret handshake." Penalties complicate grades. They muddy the water by smashing content and behavior together into a single score. I always joke that if we do that sort of thing, we must tell parents we are grading con-behave-tent (content and behavior jumbled together) during conferences. The look on their faces when we say that should tell us all we need to know.

Does it take a little bit for students to wrap their minds around seeing this new format? Of course it does, but kids are much better at understanding than we give them credit for. As with any new process, we must do it with open communication. Students need to know why it's happening and where the value is. They need to know what success will look like in this new system and what they should pay attention to. They should know what a red flag in terms of their learning would be and what they can do about it. With assessment, communication is critical, not just when we implement any sort of change, but always. If a student doesn't understand how the assessment communicates their learning progress, no matter the system, then the assessments don't matter.

The big difference, once students understand how standards-based grading works, is that they are able to experience a greater sense of control and autonomy over their learning compared to systems of grading that are essentially top-down from the teacher and not clear regarding what the student can control. This autonomy, this sense of empowerment over their success, is a key element of the motivational aspects of assessment reform.

My colleague/admin/trainer said we couldn't grade students based on behavior with standards-based grading, so how will kids be motivated to be responsible? I've truly and genuinely tried to find research that connected late work penalties to long-term increases in students' abilities to manage time and tasks, and I can't find any. The grade penalties often result in an apparent increase in work completion in the short term because kids are scared, but a frequent byproduct is that it decreases the quality of the work while increasing the likelihood that students will cheat because they are more concerned with avoiding a penalty than they are with understanding what they are doing. In effect, it eliminates the learning that was supposed to happen from whatever task we were asking them to do in the first place.

Now, just because the last paragraph mentioned not using academic penalties as consequences for behavior doesn't mean that in a standards-based system, we don't hold students accountable for productive behavior. I've found that by removing my ability to simply slap a late penalty on an assignment, I begin looking for consequences that support building better habits. For example, with my students, the two most common reasons they don't complete their work are because they are distracted (often by their phones) or they don't understand the concept (or a combination of both where they distract themselves with their phones to avoid confronting the fact that they are struggling). As such, one iteration of my late work consequence is that if a student demonstrates a pattern of not turning in work, they are assigned a late work contract where they must check their phone in with me and then spend time either during a built-in support time during the day or after school during contract hours. This consequence is designed to address the need, and it's often one that kids care a lot more about than a simple late penalty.

So, when someone says you can't hold kids accountable for behaviors that could be detrimental in the long run, what you need to tell them is this: "That's not true. You just can't do it the easy way with grade penalties, which only benefit the teacher and not the student in learning to correct the behavior." That's the actual answer. Can we hold students accountable for productive behaviors while also maintaining the academic integrity of their grades in a standards-based system? Absolutely, and in fact, I would argue that you can do so much better in a standards-based system than in a task-based one.

THE HACK IN ACTION
BY VANESSA ELLIS, MIDDLE SCHOOL SOCIAL STUDIES
TEACHER, COLUMBUS, GEORGIA

In the fall of 2017, I switched from teaching social studies at a Title I school, where I had a great relationship with my students and was successful in helping them make academic progress during their years with me, to a school that was literally and figuratively on the other side of town. One of the most striking differences was how obsessed many of my students were with their grades. And not just good grades. My students expected to make straight one hundreds.

They immediately compared grades with each other after a test. They hounded me and begged me for a few extra credit points. They tried to negotiate for a higher grade after claiming they "mis-clicked" on an assignment. It was exhausting! At my old school, I had to get the kids to care more about their grades, and at my new school, I had to get them to care less. Learning wasn't the primary goal for my new students, and I wanted them to develop a love for learning, embrace mistakes, and grow.

In addition to switching schools, I started working on my master's degree. In the summer of 2018, I took an educational trends and issues class, in which we were required to pick a current topic and write a blog series about it. After a year with grade-crazed students, I wanted to learn more about grade reform and practical ways I could shift my kids from earning to learning.

I started with my grade books. My school uses Canvas as our learning management system (LMS) and Infinite Campus as our student information system (SIS). Both platforms have grade books. All communication, assignments, and tests are administered through and graded in Canvas, but the grades that "count" are posted in Infinite Campus for each marking period. As a result, many people place importance on the grades in Infinite Campus and completely disregard the evidence of learning in Canvas.

So, my first task was to convince students and parents to prioritize Canvas over Infinite Campus. I restructured my Canvas grade book in the following ways so that students were invested in the learning process, not in arbitrary letters and numbers.

- I hid grade totals so that the average wasn't visible to students and parents. It forced them to look at the work itself rather than being satisfied with a passing average.
- The naming conventions are all based on the standard. Assignments are organized into modules based on the learning target and named accordingly. For example, *H3a Check for Understanding: Causes of the American Revolution.* This way, students can easily identify the standards they are struggling with.
- I edited assignment settings so students would have multiple attempts and the highest score was kept. I also created my own grading scheme in Canvas so the grade is displayed as either "Complete" (2/2), "Revise/Resubmit" (1/2), or "Missing" (0/2).
- I use the "New Quizzes" feature to create self-assessments in which students (1) review their work to make sure they have included the necessary components to show mastery, (2) choose from a list of things to revise, and (3) reflect over the self-assessment process and determine their own grade for the assignment.
  I provide feedback in the comments section of students' assignments. Students are expected to verify they have received and acted upon that feedback. A record of those conversations is kept on the assignment itself as well as in the Canvas inbox.

In Infinite Campus, I have a formative category weighted .01 percent and a summative category weighted 99.9 percent. The students and I work together to determine what evidence from Canvas will be placed in the formative category. I use the same naming conventions and grading scheme from Canvas so there is no confusion. This gives students, parents, and coaches a progress check of whether students are completing assignments, need to revise and resubmit, or are missing their evidence of learning. Then at the end of a marking period, students self-report the grade they believe they deserve and support their choice with evidence selected from Canvas.

Although far from perfect, these changes to my recordkeeping have positively affected my students' focus on learning. Students know that if they receive a grade of "revise/resubmit," they can do just that and improve their understanding and exhibition of learning. Because of the naming conventions and organization of tasks, students are well-versed in the language of the standards and are aware of their strengths and areas to grow. My students have risen above the shallow grabbing of points and are now doing the heavy lifting of learning and self-assessing. They don't always love it, but they do acknowledge they are better students because of it. And I'm so very proud of them.

This chapter by no means captures the entirety of transitioning to standards-based grading. I promise that some of your questions and the details will be addressed in later chapters, but here's the reality: we way overcomplicate standards-based grading. At its core, we are categorizing data based on the outcomes we hope to see with our students. Full stop. End of sentence. Period.

Yes, we eventually have to shake things up in this archaic world of education that feels like it turns so slowly, but the beauty of hacking your classroom is that you can get started on it well before the rest of the education world catches up. For my entire career, I've worked inside traditional schools with traditional grading practices, yet throughout almost the entirety of it, I've been hacking it with a standards-based approach to learning and grading in my classroom.

So often, the roadblock in people's minds with standards-based grading is that the end result will still be a grade, as if that disqualifies everything we do in our classroom to de-emphasize the grading process and emphasize the learning. That's like someone saying, "You know, I was going to eat healthy, but I have a birthday party I'm going to five months from now, and that cake's just going to ruin my diet. I'd better not start."

Yet, so often, this is the reasoning I hear as to why people won't engage in practices centered on standards-based learning. We sacrifice the 99 percent that could be good because of the 1 percent reality of the grade at the end. The entire rest of the book, all the ideas that will come in the following chapters that have completely changed how teaching and learning happen in my classroom— all of those are possible because I shifted to a standards-based approach. Do I still have to end the year with a cumulative grade for each student? Yep, but why on earth would I let that stop me? There are ways to make it work, especially if the student is an active participant in that process, which we'll talk about later, but even if the method of turning student learning in relation to standards into a final grade isn't perfect, we can make it work, minimize the harm it causes, and focus more clearly on learning along the way.

When I think back to the responses my students have given over the years about how grades and assessments have impacted them in their academic careers, and when I think about the amount of harm they tell me it's caused, how could I refuse to do something about it simply because I still have to compromise a little bit at the end of that journey?

This is the point of hacking. We may not necessarily be able to change how the journey ends, but we can make the journey so much more valuable for our students and ourselves along the way.

HACK 2

CREATE LEARNING PROGRESSIONS FOR STUDENT SUCCESS

Build Ladders to Help All Students See the Possibility of Success

Becoming isn't about arriving somewhere or achieving a certain aim. I see it instead as forward motion, a means of evolving, a way to reach continuously toward a better self. The journey doesn't end.

— MICHELLE OBAMA

THE PROBLEM: LEARNING GOALS ARE UNCLEAR, IMPRECISE, OR UNATTAINABLE

Pretend you are a ninth grade student. (I know, that may not necessarily be a time of our lives we want to relive, but just go with it for a second here.) Take it a step further: pretend you are a ninth grade student in my English Language Arts class, especially one who hasn't been super successful in previous English classes, for whom school is either literally or figuratively a foreign language. Now, with those glasses on, I want you to read the following standard:

CCSS.ELA.RL.9-10.3: Analyze how complex characters (e.g., those with multiple or conflicting motivations) develop over the course of a text, interact with other characters, and advance the plot or develop the theme.

Again, you're not your super teachery self; you're a ninth grade student who's experienced limited success and, thus, doesn't approach school with a ton of confidence. I want you to re-read that standard and ask yourself this: Where would I start to successfully demonstrate this skill?

So often, we don't acknowledge that the standard or course objective is an end goal, a destination. As educators, we can't simply give students a destination and assume that's enough for them to get there. For example, I love hiking. I go hiking solo a lot. My wife hates this part, but I have a terrible sense of direction. If you just gave me a destination and told me to get there, I would end up walking around in the woods for a while before giving up and returning to my car, disappointed and feeling like I just wasted a bunch of time (if I were lucky).

Now, let's compare that to an alternative. Say you gave me a destination and then handed me a topographical map of the trail. Not only would I get there, but I could check my progress along the way and feel good about what I was doing. Not only that but when I was exhausted and feeling like I couldn't make it, I would be able to see how close I was to that next waypoint and use that to find the discretionary effort I needed to push to the next level.

When I first started using a standards-based approach, I focused too much on the destination and didn't realize that there were kids at the start of this "hike" asking how to get to the top, and all I did was continue pointing to the top. I just kept focusing on the destination without realizing some kids didn't even know where the trailhead was.

Before I make everyone think that clarity in our end goals isn't important—please know that it absolutely is. If I can't clearly point out the end goal, no one's going to get there, but that can't be the only thing we do. This is where backward planning got its start. We realized how important it is to clearly identify the goal, but the way I was taught to backward plan was to build the assessments first and then the activities. I was never taught how to meaningfully backward plan the learning. What I mean is that no one ever talked to me about how to think through the sequence of learning that I would be teaching—the knowledge, content, and skills—that would lead students to successfully reach the standard identified in the curriculum.

Now, before someone jumps in and yells about how learning is not one-size-fits-all and that no one knows how each individual brain will function—I am aware that we can't script out a sequence for every student to follow. I was a student who liked to skip around. In my professional life, I still love to skip around and then figure out the pieces I missed along the way. Learning is messy. Anyone who tells you otherwise is selling you a lie.

However, I will say that if a student never learns what nouns and verbs are, it will be hard to talk to them about how to make a complete sentence. If a student never learns what concrete objects and abstract ideas are, it will be hard for them to grasp symbolism. If a student never learns to multiply, you might as well just kiss exponents goodbye.

I often think about this in my life. I absolutely love building things. One of my first solo building projects was a doghouse. Here's the thing, though. I wasn't just thrown into a wood shop and told, "Make a doghouse." People showed me how a miter saw worked. I learned basic geometry to help cut the right angles. I learned about different materials that I could use for the doghouse.

Everything we do involves hidden content knowledge and skills that, as teachers, are our job to think through for our students. Do we expect every student to follow every step along the way? No. We're not making this a one-size-fits-all system. We're making a series of waypoints students can look to when they get lost. We're making a guiding document so that when a student sees the destination and thinks, "I can't do it," I can point out the next, much closer step and say, "Let's just get here first."

THE HACK:
CREATE LEARNING PROGRESSIONS
FOR STUDENT SUCCESS

Let's talk about how learning progressions are better for your students (and you) than rubrics. First, know that I don't hate rubrics; I just think they are too often used for the wrong purpose. Do they have value? Absolutely, but only when used at the right time. Think about the rubric in Image 2.1.

1 (BEGINNING)	2 (DEVELOPING)	3 (APPLYING)	4 (EXTENDING)
I struggle to make complete sentences.	I frequently make mistakes in end-of-sentence punctuation.	I occasionally make mistakes in end-of-sentence punctuation.	I make no mistakes in end-of-sentence punctuation.

Image 2.1: A rubric example.

It would be a common rubric you might see in an ELA classroom. Now, think about the answers to these two questions: (1) When is this tool valuable? (2) Who is it valuable for?

We'll start with the teacher perspective. Is this a valuable tool at the beginning of a unit of study? Possibly, because it could help to clarify the end goal. What about at the end of a unit of study, especially for assessing student demonstrations of learning? Absolutely. In fact, several studies point to well-designed rubrics with intentional calibration through norming, discussing how the rubric should be interpreted, and helping align expectations within teams to promote fairness in grading practices. For teachers, rubrics are especially valuable at the end of the learning process when assessing student demonstrations of learning.

Let's switch to the student perspective, and I want to work backward here. Are rubrics valuable for students at the end of a unit, maybe when they are about to start a big project or when they are revising? The answer is yes, probably. Here are key pros and cons of the student use of rubrics around assessments:

▶ **Pro: It can increase the accuracy of peer- and self-assessment.** When students are asked to self- or peer-assess, providing a rubric paired with exemplars has been shown to increase the accuracy of student assessment and the quality of feedback in peer-feedback activities (Jonsson and Svingby 2007).

▶ **Pro: It decreases the impact of implicit bias.** In an infamous study, multiple teachers were given the same piece of writing, but in some, the names were all stereotypically White-sounding names, while others had stereotypically Black-sounding names. Papers with Black-sounding names were scored lower than those with the White-sounding names, despite the writing being identical (Quinn 2020).

You may say, "But this sounds like we're talking about the teacher again." Correct, but here's why I'm putting it in this section. In John Hattie's widely-referenced work around visible learning, he identifies a huge list of classroom elements that have an impact on learning. If you look at all the effects he lists, one of the biggest impacts on student achievement is what he calls "Student Self-Reported Grades," but the simpler way of saying it is "Student Expectations."

As such, using rubrics to increase the accuracy of any scores we provide to students ends up being a crucial part of the student's future learning because if bias deflates student scores, that can impact their identity and belief in their ability to be successful, thus hindering their motivation. So, is it valuable for the student to have a rubric in place when they demonstrate their learning? Absolutely.

- **Con:** One downside of a rubric is that it can be limiting. It narrows the scope of success for many students, often limiting how they demonstrate their understanding. In essence, rubrics often take away the possibility of creativity and control, which can be a motivating factor for students. This doesn't mean all rubrics are bad, but it's a facet we must keep in mind as we implement rubrics.

If we want students to be motivated, we must focus on helping them see the possibility and the path to success.

Now we get to the part that I really want us to think about: What is the usefulness of rubrics at the beginning of a learning process (or even during the learning process) for students? Go back to the mind of our hypothetical struggling ninth grade student, and turn back to read Image 2.1 again as if it's being introduced to you for the first time.

Where do you, the student, begin? Where is your access point to the learning? The only on-ramp to success in this rubric is that you must already know what a complete sentence is. That's the one way you can be successful based on this rubric, and from there, it's just different degrees of success in that one way. Again, think about this as the student who never understood subjects and verbs, the student who just moved here and is trying to navigate school in a new language, or the student who's always gotten marks that they use fragments and run-ons but never understood what that means. Where do they get to see themselves in this rubric, and, more importantly, do they see a path to success to grow their motivation?

The answer is that they don't, and as a result, the cost-benefit ratio is completely out of whack because the route to success is filled with hurdles they don't understand. In the context of learning, the cost-benefit ratio usually means that if a student sees success as a gigantic leap that they aren't sure they can even do (seen as a high cost), it is likely the learning (the benefit) will not seem valuable enough to outweigh the cost they would have to invest to get there, which can crush motivation to engage in that process. When the access point to success is just one spot, we end up seeing students who disengage or are unmotivated. Call it what you want, but the reality is this is what they feel they need to do to preserve their dignity.

If we want students to be motivated, we must focus on helping them see the possibility and the path to success. To illustrate this, contrast the two examples in Image 2.1 (a rubric example) and Image 2.2 (a learning progression example).

1 (BEGINNING)	2 (DEVELOPING)	3 (APPLYING)	4 (EXTENDING)
I struggle to make complete sentences.	I frequently make mistakes in end-of-sentence punctuation.	I occasionally make mistakes in end-of-sentence punctuation.	I make no mistakes in end-of-sentence punctuation.

Image 2.1: A rubric example.

BEGINNING	DEVELOPING	APPROACHING	APPLYING	EXTENDING
I can define subjects and verbs and identify them in sentences.	I can define independent and dependent clauses and identify them when given examples.	I can write simple sentences with one subject and one verb.	I can write simple sentences with compound subjects and/or compound verbs.	I can write compound or complex sentences by combining independent and/or dependent clauses.

Image 2.2: A learning progression example.

Go back to our example student, that ninth grader who's not too thrilled to be in an English classroom. The goal is still the same. Even though one goal is to evaluate your ability to write a complete sentence and the other is to understand the steps of how to write a complete sentence and the building blocks needed along the way, we're still focused on how to write a complete sentence in both. However, notice the on-ramps to the learning in the learning progression. If I don't even know what a subject and verb are, there's a place for me in this progression. Maybe I already know those, but I don't know what an independent clause is. Well, I also have a place to access the learning and get on the path to success.

I know we cannot say for certain that every student needs to follow this path to be successful in the skill, but not providing any ideas around how to get started in the learning journey ends up privileging kids with background knowledge because they already possess the knowledge we assume they should have coming in. When we make that assumption and then start there, we often keep the rest of the kids from being able to begin their learning journeys from wherever they are.

The idea is that we are thinking back through what a student would need to learn to be successful with this concept, and then we are identifying those pieces of knowledge or skills students can focus on one at a time. This process of unpacking was difficult for me at first, but here's how I've come to look at my progressions.

The first level or two are often just the terms or concepts students need to be aware of, and usually for the first level, I will go below what people would consider to be at grade level. Using the prior example, knowing what subjects and verbs are is absolutely not in the ninth grade standards, but not knowing them means students won't be able to understand a discussion around complete sentences. We can bemoan the fact that they don't know it, wailing and gnashing our teeth that "they were supposed to learn this in elementary school." That might make us feel good to blow off some steam, but it doesn't change the fact that there are kids in our rooms who don't know the basics and who won't be successful unless they learn them.

For me, that's the point of these first few levels. I ask myself, "What is the background knowledge students need to come into this with to be able to take it to the next level?" Doing this is crucial in helping me understand how to differentiate effectively in my classroom. When I initially heard "differentiation," I thought it meant that I had to prepare a different project for each student to do, but what I've learned through the integration of learning progressions in my classroom is that it's not about giving students different projects; it's about helping students see the different levels of learning complexity clearly enough to articulate what they need and how to access resources at their disposal to pursue the goals.

Prior to integrating learning progressions into how students experience my class, I felt guilty by providing a goal without ensuring everyone saw a place to start. Some students looked at it and immediately perceived success as an impossibility. Using my hiking analogy again, it was basically the equivalent of me telling a student, "See that peak? That's where you're going," but then when they asked where the trailhead began, I just dropped them off at the side of the road and told them to figure it out.

The same situation often happens with students and their motivation. It takes confidence to willingly engage in productive struggle, and if students haven't found a learning goal where their success is a possibility, how are they supposed to build that confidence?

The next levels encompass the application of those concepts in practice. Using the prior example, once students know what subjects, verbs, dependent clauses, and independent clauses are, then we start using them. Again, this isolation allows students to focus on one concept at a time, and the point of the progression is that it's clear how they all will fit together and build toward a set of knowledge and skills at the end.

The application phase is where students begin to see how the work they did in the first couple of steps builds toward a deeper understanding. We've taken the terms they learned in isolation and started putting them into practice. This makes their theoretical knowledge more practical. It's no longer just learning *about* the concepts; it's learning *how to use them*. However, the scope of how these steps use the concepts is still somewhat limited.

The last steps of the progression are where I focus on broadening how these concepts are applied. For example, the final step of our progression combines the concepts and what students practiced in new ways. For this, instead of writing simple sentences, now we're combining multiple simple sentences together or even a simple sentence with a dependent clause to make a complex sentence.

In other progressions, I focus on how this skill combines with another we've previously learned. For example, in a progression on character development, the final step has students thinking about how character development contributes to thematic development in a text. Once they've understood a concept and started using it, a good next step is to help them understand what it looks like when they use that skill most effectively.

It's important to stop here and address that a key element of making this type of differentiation possible in the classroom is to leverage asynchronous resources. Pre-recorded lessons, YouTube videos, and curated content go a long way toward addressing different phases of the progression with different students at different times.

In short, here's how I think about the phases of a learning progression.

1. **Background knowledge and terms.** Ensure the foundational elements are there. In this phase, I ask myself, "What do students need to know to be able to engage in conversations and lessons around the topic or skill?"

2. **Application of content.** Once students feel confident about the concepts and content, they can start putting them into practice. At this stage, I ask myself, "If I were just starting out, what's the simplest way I could put this into practice?"

3. **Integration of content and skills.** Apply content in complex situations and in connection with other concepts. I often ask, "What would this look like in the real world?"

I have seen so many teachers use learning progressions in different ways, but here's how I use them with my students. At the beginning of each unit, students get a unit guide that has the learning progressions listed, space for them to record any scores from assessments, space for feedback, and space for reflection. Students mark off where they are and what they think they know already. Then, after every assessment or two, we pause to go back to the learning progression to record our data and feedback, write down what we know and learned, and update our progress. Then, at the end of the unit, we can use the data to sit down and talk about their cumulative scores for the unit of study.

I've seen teachers who are intentional about portfolios use learning progressions incredibly well. In the portfolio, students attach the learning progression to their best work to demonstrate their growth, sometimes explaining how their work shows their learning in a little memo in the portfolio.

I've also seen teachers use these learning progressions by designing HyperRubrics, which are essentially a learning progression that has digital resources linked directly into the progression to support independent learning. While this could result in locking students into the progression as just a scripted series of activities, if done well, it can increase ownership for students through clarity and resources.

Again, the goal with all of this—learning progressions and implementing a more standards-based assessment practice—is to change how teaching and learning happen in our rooms, ideally creating scenarios where students have the clarity and confidence they need to feel motivated by the possibility of growth and success.

Learning progressions made a huge difference in my classroom, both in how learning happens and in how motivated students are to attempt learning, no matter where they're starting from. They haven't made that difference on their own. As with standards-based grading, learning progressions open doors for incredible student engagement with the learning. (For more student engagement strategies, see the book *Even More Hacking Engagement* by James Sturtevant.) This is where hacking motivation through assessment must start. We can't superficially change what we do and then ask why nothing meaningful shifted. We must start the hack by questioning the foundation, and if we can't change the foundation at a broader county or district level, we at least have the power to shift at the micro level in our classrooms.

WHAT YOU CAN DO TOMORROW

The greatest aspect of learning progressions is that there are a million ways to use them, and they don't require you to overhaul everything. You can gradually implement them or use them for one-off activities to feel out how they can work for you and your students in context. Keep your courage up even if students don't take to them right away. They're new and weird for students, especially when students are conditioned by a system that often tells them to do tasks for points. It's like they consider learning progressions as wolves in sheep's clothing that will end up giving them a bad grade. So, try to avoid attaching points to learning progressions and activities connected with them as much as possible. When points are mixed in, they immediately become the focus. What should be a measure of growth becomes the goal, so it's my mission to minimize the impact and use of points around learning progressions.

▶ **Talk to a teacher a grade level below you.** The biggest problem I run into when thinking about how to teach a concept is being completely unaware of the previous year's instruction that I might build upon in my instruction. This problem is twofold, though. First, I often assume a skill was covered when it really wasn't. I'd see the curriculum guide from the previous year and foolishly think, "Yep, they definitely covered all of this," while knowing I don't cover my entire curriculum guide, either. Second, I often assume that because it was taught, it was learned. This results in learning gaps. Talking to the previous teacher helps me home in on exactly what fits in the earlier steps of a learning progression.

▶ **Explore resources related to unpacking standards.** Educators can find countless resources about unpacking standards. Various approaches will be different than I outlined in this chapter, but no matter what, the goal is to make the standards clear and more approachable. It can be daunting in the beginning, especially as you start thinking about unpacking all your standards and building learning progressions. However, if you spend time reading about how to unpack standards and looking at examples, you'll feel more confident going into it. As a bonus, you'll be much faster at it, too. Two of my favorite places to go regarding this topic are Learning Sciences International and the Ohio Department of Education's Learning Standards Extended.

▶ **Ask your colleagues, "What does this standard ask students to do?"** This conversation can be one of the most valuable ways we begin the process of building progressions, and it's incredibly valuable for a team to do together. If you don't have a team within your school, reach out on social networks to have this conversation with other educators teaching the same subjects as you.

Taking our standards and asking what they expect students to know and do is a foundational piece of building the clarity that students need to feel like they can be successful, which is a key component of motivation in the classroom.

A BLUEPRINT FOR FULL IMPLEMENTATION

STEP 1   STEP 2   STEP 3   STEP 4   STEP 5

Identify priority standards with your grade-level or content-specific team.

Some of the most valuable conversations with my PLCs in the past were around this concept, and they were guided by this question: "What do we want students to understand deeply?" This is at the heart of identifying priority standards. We're thinking about our values in terms of what matters most for students to get out of education, we're thinking about the long-term success of our students and what they need, and then we're thinking about how we want to prioritize our values in the curriculum.

While many have published details about how to identify priority standards, Larry Ainsworth's work on this topic has been the most valuable to me. He shares three key elements to focus on when identifying priority standards: endurance, leverage, and readiness. Let's go over each one in more detail.

▶ **Endurance:** How useful is this skill outside of an academic setting? How useful is it for life in general?

- Example: Learning to analyze figurative language is fun in an ELA class, but learning to evaluate a source of information to determine its reliability would have a higher endurance score when choosing priority standards.

▶ **Leverage:** How useful is it in multiple different content areas? What is the general academic value of the standard?

- Example: I love getting to teach characterization and character development with my students (mostly because it's fun to hear them come back and talk about how they are analyzing all their friends now), but teaching them how to support a claim with evidence will serve them well in multiple classrooms.

▶ **Readiness:** How necessary is the skill or concept in their success in subsequent classes or content? How much does the skill support the learning of later or more complex skills in the same content area?

- Example: Identifying subjects and verbs might not necessarily be useful in other content areas, and it might not seem like a skill you'd use in the real world, but in helping students learn to write more complex sentences or identify errors in their writing, they must first know that basic skill.

With these three categories, it's not a yes or no rating. Think of it more like a sliding scale, and then try to figure out how high or low a standard would fall on the scale. In choosing priority standards, you're looking for those that have higher marks in as many of those categories as possible. It's difficult, especially when we may feel like every detail is crucial for students to know. For me, it's always been helpful to get outside opinions, both from teachers outside my school in the same content area through a professional learning network (X is my go-to these days) and from teachers in my building in different content areas. It helps me see the situation from a different perspective, and that often helps me identify priority standards.

The goal in identifying priority standards isn't to say which knowledge and skills students will be exposed to or engage in. Rather, it's to identify which standards get explicit instruction, intentional assessment, and targeted intervention to ensure students learn the content fully and can apply the skills. We still engage in the rest of the standards but in a less intensive way. I used to think this meant I would have to deprioritize concepts or that they wouldn't get noticed in the classroom. While this might be

Sometimes, by not measuring data, we're creating space to explore it in more meaningful (but less quantifiable) ways.

the case sometimes, more often, there's much more joy in the non-emphasized standards because we simply get to enjoy them. We don't have to quantify anything. Sometimes, by not measuring data, we're creating space to explore it in more meaningful (but less quantifiable) ways.

STEP 1   STEP 2   STEP 3   STEP 4   STEP 5

Analyze your standards.

Standards are often unclear about what precisely should be taught and learned. They provide a general goal as to what students should be able to do, but that doesn't help anyone understand what they need to learn to get there, at least on the surface. When there is a goal without a clear path to reach it, it can often dampen motivation because of confusion or a lack of confidence about the possibility of success.

Fortunately, there's an easy trick that can make unpacking standards so much faster and clearer. Here's the trick: Annotate the standard by marking all the verbs one way and all the nouns another. Let's look at an example using the same standard from the beginning of this chapter.

CCSS.ELA.RL.9-10.3: Analyze how complex characters (e.g., those with multiple or conflicting motivations) develop over the course of a text, interact with other characters, and advance the plot or develop the theme.

Step one is to identify the nouns in the standard, especially focusing on the ones that have content-specific meanings. In the following example, all the nouns are underlined.

CCSS.ELA.RL.9-10.3: Analyze how complex characters (e.g., those with multiple or conflicting motivations) develop over the *course* of a *text*, interact with other characters, and advance the plot or develop the theme.

By doing this, we now have a list of the concepts students need to learn to reach this goal. We can break down what complex characters are (round versus flat, static versus dynamic). We know that students must understand plot and theme, which could be background knowledge to refresh. In identifying the nouns, we are identifying the specific content students need to learn. (Note: *course* and *text* are italicized because not every noun will be a concept we must teach or address, so they are set apart from the rest.)

The next step is to highlight the verbs. The following example shows the verbs identified in bold.

CCSS.ELA.RL.9-10.3: **Analyze** how complex characters (e.g., those with multiple or conflicting motivations) **develop** over the *course* of a *text*, **interact** with other characters, and **advance** the plot or **develop** the theme.

This process helps us identify the **skills students need to practice**. Essentially, the nouns are the parts, and the verbs are what students do with them.

I found it more helpful to add one more step to this process. Now that we have our nouns (concepts) identified and our verbs (skills) noted, I found it helpful to package these back into student-ready "I can" statements. Not only does it help to clarify what students will be learning, but the "I can" form can also be useful for students. For example, I might take the noun complex characters and turn it into an "I can" statement like this: "I can explain how authors create complex characters and the methods they use to develop them."

Build learning progressions.

Once you have the pieces of essential learning figured out, it's time to think about sequencing and scaffolding to provide access to the learning. As a reminder, learning progressions are more guidelines than rules. I can't look at a student and tell you precisely how they will learn the content. No one can. What we can do is understand that building blocks are helpful to know before moving on to the next step, and it's our job to make students aware of those steps. If nothing else, the student can return to them after they've tried their own route if they need to figure out where they went wrong or why they're stuck.

With that in mind, let's look at how to build the progressions. To do this, put yourself in the mindset of our ninth grade student again. We know that the essential learning is "I can explain how authors create complex characters and the methods they use to develop them," but where do we start? Remember, this student doesn't have the background knowledge we have as educators. They don't have the confidence that we have to take risks in learning and be comfortable with the unknown.

See Image 2.3 to understand what the overall progression could look like, and then I will explain the thinking behind each phase.

ESSENTIAL LEARNING	PHASE 1	PHASE 2	PHASE 3	PHASE 4	PHASE 5
I can explain how authors create complex characters and the methods they use to develop them.	I can explain what conflict is, what major elements of plot are, and what protagonists and antagonists are.	I can explain what static and dynamic characters are, and I can describe the methods of characterization an author might use to develop them.	When given a specific character, I can explain which methods of characterization are used to develop them.	I can explain how a character changes or develops by analyzing the methods of characterization, focusing specifically on what causes them to change.	I can explain how a character's development helps to make a theme more complex.

Image 2.3: Character development learning progression.

In the first phase of a progression, I focus on the background vocabulary and concepts students will need as background knowledge when engaged in discussions around this piece of essential learning. The goal at this stage is to ensure any potential gaps in previous learning are explicit for all students. When we forget to identify these crucial starting points, students who don't have the vocabulary will feel confused, behind, or unconfident. This becomes problematic for motivation. When we help students feel competent, it spurs them into a cycle of motivation, and the opposite can also be true. When a student starts by feeling incompetent and not having the opportunity to remedy that, it lowers their confidence, which creates a cycle with a lack of motivation, which many people call learned helplessness.

If possible, talk with teachers of the grade level before yours. This dialogue allows you to hear what they taught and what they didn't so you know what background knowledge students gained. Also, these progressions are often vehicles to help build vertical coherence from grade to grade.

In the second phase, I often focus on the new vocabulary and concepts being introduced. The goal is to prioritize the most important new pieces and not throw too much at students all at once to avoid potential cognitive overload. Look for the high-leverage words and concepts students need as a foundation.

Phase three is what I call the "training wheels on" phase. Here, my goal is to create a controlled environment with as few moving pieces as possible to isolate the application of the skill. I'm not tracking growth or even analyzing much. I'm simply taking the new concept and trying it out in a controlled environment. If we increase the complexity too quickly, it will be difficult for the student to experience success. The goal here is that students can have an experience of success in a controlled environment before moving forward. Think about phase three as bowling with bumpers. How do we minimize the risk in the learning while still allowing them to engage in new concepts to build their motivation through experiences of growth?

In phase four, the training wheels come off. Now we're creating space for students to analyze these specific elements within the full context of whatever we're working with. More specifically, they are thinking beyond just the surface. If phase three is about explaining the concept in isolation, phase four is about exploring the concept in its full context.

There is still an element that focuses on the methods of characterization, but there's slightly less guidance about what to focus on. More moving pieces are at play now. The key, though, is that it is still focused on the one skill the student is learning. We aren't pulling anything new into the mix yet. We're just focused on the piece of essential learning.

For phase five, if we want the learning to stick and be retained for the long term, we must help students build as many pathways as possible around this information. We can think about it in two ways. First, we can focus on working with the new information in a novel context. Second, we can focus on drawing connections between what we're learning now and other information we've learned previously.

With characterization, this might be where I bring in the final part of the standard, which focuses on connecting it to a theme in a literary text, an idea we've previously studied. Not only does this create connections with the new content, but it also spirals back to a previous piece of learning, better cementing those pathways and making it more likely that information will be retained, too.

Sometimes, we overthink learning progressions. Simplifying the process of learning a new concept is the goal. We create a map so that, no matter where students are in the journey, when they get lost, they can find their way again. When we can set them up with this process and structure to take their learning into their own hands and be successful with it, that's when we know we're laying the groundwork for motivation to blossom.

Determine how to use the learning progressions.

The best explanation I can offer for how to use learning progressions is to think of them as a map. If you're going on a hike, you use the map at the beginning to do some planning, but then you consult it multiple times throughout the hike when you're unsure of where to go next or worried you're off track.

Learning progressions function the same way. When I begin a new unit of study, the class starts by examining the learning progressions. I've found it helps to have exemplars available that we can look at together to explain what the concepts in the progression look like as an end product. It helps to ground the students a bit more and give them a clearer understanding of where we're headed while we initially examine the progressions.

Once we've discussed them, my goal is to have a diagnostic students can use to figure out where they're starting. This may be a quick quiz, a self-assessment, or even just a brainstorm of all that they know about the skill going into it. The tricky part with this phase is that it is possible for students to feel discouraged if they are starting at a different spot from their peers, and if we leave that alone, it has the potential to harm their motivation. To remedy this and help shift their mindset, I try to have time early on for students to get a quick win from their progression. For students starting at the earlier phases of the progression, that may mean simply getting a new definition they didn't know before. The key is that once I see the student experience success, no matter the level, I make sure to point out that their effort led to growth. This helps get students in a mindset that is focused on their capacity for success instead of what they may view as a deficit in starting at an earlier phase.

While the launch is important, the most value I see in my classroom with the learning progressions is in their function as a reflective tool during the learning process. We can use them effectively in two ways.

First, before we jump into a learning experience for the day, I ask students to get out their learning progressions and identify where they are and what they need to learn next. This helps build motivation because it gives a purpose to the learning, and it reminds them that their next steps to success are not far off. While nothing is foolproof, this centers the students a lot more than my old approach of just putting the success criteria on the board for everyone, as that often set the bar either too far ahead for some students or too far behind for others.

Second, my classes use them during the learning as a reflection tool after an assessment. Earlier, I mentioned that rubrics and progressions work well together, and this is where those two intersect. After the students attempt to demonstrate their learning, we'll often use a rubric to evaluate the attempt. This might be a self-assessment, peer evaluation, or other learning I've assessed. However, we don't stop there. Students reevaluate where they are in their progressions based on the feedback they received, questions they got wrong on a quiz, or other tracking methods. Using that information, they will set new intentions for their learning.

This process and the language I use around it focus on one thing: celebration. Some students will see themselves grow and move along the learning progressions in these moments, and we can celebrate their growth. Other students might not be ready to move along yet, but we can still celebrate that they knew what to try for and they took an academic risk to go for it. It's crucial that the language used in this process emphasizes how their effort is helping them make progress. Helping them connect effort with progress is one of the best ways to build self-efficacy—the ability to see themselves as successful. As we've talked about all along, the ability to see themselves as successful is one of the core elements of motivation.

STEP 1   STEP 2   STEP 3   STEP 4   STEP 5

Use them, use them, use them.

As someone who is skeptical about overusing methods in the classroom and making them too mundane so they lose their effectiveness, I've never once felt like I've used the learning progressions too much. They're such a grounding force for students and me that they've become the backbone of my classroom. The visual cue that tells me if I'm using them well in my instruction is that I see students using them even when I haven't asked.

They're great for entry tasks, exit tickets, and processing breaks. I say, "Take out your learning progressions and explain to your partner one thing you've learned that has moved you along your progression." I can follow up by asking a few students to share, and then we all get to celebrate their learning.

No matter how you use them in the classroom, this needs to be the focus of the learning progressions. They need to help students see where they're demonstrating competence so they can build the confidence they need to move to the next phase. It's in the cultivation of this confidence that they tap into motivation.

OVERCOMING PUSHBACK

Here are a few common types of concerns for this Hack and how to address them.

What about the students who are behind their peers in the progression? Won't they feel bad? Kids are more socially savvy than we give them credit for. So yes, they will know they are behind their peers, but we can attempt to take the negative feelings out of it. First, we talk often about how no one can be good at everything. I try to model this for them. I let them know that I didn't get great grades in my English class when I was in high school. I show them pictures of me learning to use a new camera. I talk about all the numerous house projects I've done that showed I didn't know what I was doing.

We can help them break out of the mold that tells them perfection is everything, and we can model it and share how we still struggle as a learner, too. We can show them there's more value and meaning in being willing to be bad at something and admitting we have growing to do than there is in pretending to be perfect all the time. We owe it to them to have those hard conversations, to model what it looks like, and to celebrate learning in our classrooms.

What if students only get to the first couple of phases in the progression? Won't that trap them in low-level learning experiences? If you've read some of the critiques of Bloom's taxonomy, you know this is the biggest issue that arises, and it's often problematic in classrooms that adhere too strictly to the model. No, we don't want students simply memorizing and regurgitating, and our students who struggle the most often get trapped in this spot if we aren't careful.

Now, do they need to learn the vocabulary before they can make leaps and bounds? Yes, the early steps are important. Too often, we hurry through the set curriculum and don't ensure that all students have the language they need to take part in the conversation. They need a checkpoint to make sure they know the concepts and vocabulary, but that doesn't mean it's all they should be able to do. Students can spend part of their learning time focused on these foundational understandings, but we should also be ensuring that they get to experience the more interesting side of the content, too, whether that's through creating a project, working on a collaboration with peers, or simply engaging in meaningful discussions on the bigger factors that make the curriculum meaningful.

Going back to my experience in learning photography, I didn't just sit around, reading about how to take photos. I started taking photos, and along the way, I learned the concepts. Taking photos gave me a reason to learn the content. I'd take a photo of a bird in flight, but its wings were blurry, so I'd learn about shutter speed. I'd take a portrait of my dog, but the background was in focus, so I'd research aperture.

For students who struggle the most and don't enjoy school, we want to focus on creating experiences that make the learning more meaningful and relevant. Once students have had experiences that make the content interesting, then they will be more willing to engage in the mundane yet essential pieces of the learning process.

This seems like so much work! How am I supposed to do this for all my standards? First, don't do this for all your standards. To use learning progressions well and have the time for reflection, multiple attempts, and individualized pacing, you can't have a million of them. For a trimester (twelve weeks), I usually have anywhere from five to ten learning progressions—seven seems to be the sweet spot—into which we dive deeply. This is why the process of identifying priority standards is so important. In my classroom, we still learn about the elements not identified as priority standards, but we don't focus on growth with them as we do on the priority standards.

Second, this process is best done in collaboration with others. When you sit down with someone else to talk through it, the brainstorming speeds up and it helps you to avoid missing key pieces. Getting more diverse perspectives and opinions will always make the finished product better. This might mean you take some of your department meeting time to discuss this, or maybe you reach out to others via social networks to collaborate.

Making assessment more valuable, meaningful, and equitable needs the momentum of multiple people behind it. I've seen schools create incredible outcomes that snowball because one teacher reached out to a couple people and then those people reached out to more people, and before you know it, the school decides to get rid of a harmful practice entirely so it can embrace a more student-centered one. For your sake and the sake of change, don't always try to go it alone.

What about students on IEPs or those who require modified grading? How does this benefit them and work well with their IEPs? This is another area where learning progressions can be incredibly valuable. In fact, the original document that got me using learning progressions in the classroom was called Ohio's Learning Standards – Extended (OLS-E). This document broke down all the standards to work backward to find appropriate goals for students at different levels to provide more scaffolding. This inspiration led me to start thinking about why we don't do this for every single classroom.

Let's say you have a student in your classroom who qualifies for services in reading. You know they are not quite ready for the content the class is moving toward. Learning progressions can support you in a couple of ways to differentiate for this student. First, you already have the content itself differentiated. While phase four might be the "goal" for the class, you can shift where that goal is along the learning process. Maybe the goal is phase three for this student.

Second, because the content is separated from the task, you can adapt the context the student will be working in to demonstrate their understanding of the goals. For example, if all my students will be reading a text that is inaccessible for one student, I can pull that student aside to talk about their independent reading and use that to get evidence for where they are in the learning progression.

When I started working with learning progressions, I realized that clarity was the key to flexibility. When I precisely know what students need to learn, I can teach the content in different ways. The goal here is that we should always be looking for access points. We're all on the same journey, but learning progressions allow us to create different places for students to start.

THE HACK IN ACTION
BY ANGELA STOCKMAN AND KELLY CASTLE,
INSTRUCTIONAL DESIGNERS, DAEMEN UNIVERSITY,
AMHERST, NEW YORK

Angela Stockman became interested in HyperRubrics (an extension of a learning progression where you embed technology resources to further the learning) as a writing teacher who was beginning to understand the potential for rubrics to serve as learning instruments rather than evaluative devices.

Jennifer Borgioli Binis, an education researcher and author, aims to mitigate these tensions through her ongoing development of the Quality Rubrics Wiki, a tool that many educators might appreciate tucking into their digital pockets. She offers an informed definition of quality rubrics, clarity around their dimensions and how to develop them, and an entire collection of protocols and resources that support design and revision.

Still, as Peter Schilke, director of instructional design for Daemen University, often reminds us, it's not the wand but the wizard that determines the quality of any magic we might practice, and when it comes to the development and implementation of high-quality rubrics, truer words could not be spoken.

Rubrics can truly make or break a learning experience.

This is why we fell in love with the HyperRubric.

As a Quality Matters institution, Daemen University is committed to continuous improvement in online learning. Instructors who choose to work with our office around the implementation of Quality Matters Standards are often daunted by the demands of these forty-two outcomes, and those who are new to online learning often struggle to define what "good" looks like, how to get there, and how to grow far beyond it.

We're discovering that hyperlinked learning progressions serve online course designers well. Consider the example in Image 2.4, which represents the way in which one of the instructors we support might pursue Quality Matters Specific Review Standard 5.2: *Learning activities promote opportunities for interaction that support active learning.*

Notice how the descriptors rely upon progressive language that articulates what a course designer might do to pursue and then exceed Quality Matters expectations. While the QM rubric offers our instructors a robust definition of what it looks like to meet their standards, our hyperlinked learning progression reflects what a course designer might do as they're beginning to meet the standard, progressing toward it, meeting it, and exceeding it. And there is more to it: Using hyperlinked progressions enables us to embed deeper professional learning opportunities within the tool so that the instructors we serve may learn much more about the promising practices—or even, as in this case—factors that should give us pause before we choose to pick them up.

Quality Matters Specific Review Standard 5.2: Learning activities promote opportunities for interaction that support active learning	BEGINNING	APPROACHING	MEETING	EXCEEDING
	Require learners to apply what they learned from each week's video lectures to an auto-graded quiz. This promotes learner-content engagement.	Expect learners to engage in a weekly quality online discussion about the assigned reading. This promotes learner-content & learner-learner engagement.	Create a "muddiest points" discussion board. Learners share their points of confusion. Their peers & teacher help to clarify their thinking. This creates learner-content, learner-learner, & learner-instructor engagement.	Analyze topics shared most often in the "muddiest points" board & use these findings to inform instruction. Learners receive quick support, and it is a powerful formative assessment approach that improves instruction and student learning outcomes.

Image 2.4: Quality Matters HyperRubric.

Instructors who choose to work with our office around the implementation of Quality Matters Standards are now introduced to the protocol questions shown in Image 2.5. As we work through it together, learning progressions come to life as the codesigned product of a creative and collaborative effort.

Image 2.5: Protocol questions.

The course design process is often complicated by perceived power imbalances and tensions surrounding course quality and how it might reflect upon course designers—especially those who are new to this work. Our office is constantly seeking new ways to build and sustain truly collegial relationships with course builders of all capacity levels, and using our protocol to co-construct hyperlinked learning progressions with the instructors we serve definitely helps us bridge this divide. It's not just the tool but the process itself that decenters us as facilitators and deepens our collective expertise. We're looking forward to seeing how our hyperlinked learning progressions help us pursue the standards of quality course design in increasingly creative and diverse ways.

If a genie pops out of a bottle and says to me, "Of all the changes you've made to your assessment practices, you only get to keep one. Which one will it be?" I can say with confidence that I would hold on to learning progressions.

The magic isn't within the progressions themselves but in the fact that they've changed how I gather evidence from my students. They've opened conversations about learning and facilitated conversations about final grades that make those processes more student-centered, transforming kids into active participants in those processes instead of passive recipients of information and grades.

Previously, I tried to increase the ownership in my classroom, but like you may have felt, it went sideways quickly. Students were lost and confused; some just gave up altogether. I hate to admit it, but I blamed the students. I thought to myself, "They just aren't mature enough to handle it," or "All they care about is the easy way out." What I learned is that the foundation for meaningful ownership is clarity. When we've provided clarity, then students feel confident about what is needed or expected so they can approach it in their own way. When we've provided small benchmarks, students can build their confidence by celebrating their competence, and through this process, we can get the snowball of motivation rolling because it helps students see their capacity for success.

Learning progressions are about unpacking standards, yes, but they are even more about shifting the power in the classroom. When we view ourselves as the arbiter of knowledge or the sage on the stage all the time, students will act in accordance, becoming complacent to just sit in their chairs while we do our thing. However, when we say, "Here. I've done everything I can to show you the way, and I'm giving it to you. What are you going to do with this?" we communicate to the students that we trust them and believe they can learn on their own. We show them we care just as much or more about the journey and the process as we do about the end goal. We let them know they are just as important in this classroom as we are and that their brains are capable of incredible discoveries on their own.

This is a consistent thread throughout this book: The key isn't in simply adding another tool to your toolbelt. The key is to understand the function and purpose of the tool. Learning progressions are the tool, but the "why" behind them is what matters. The goal is to develop background elements that support an increase in student ownership in the classroom. We're creating an environment that allows students the chance to see their success and to build upon it. By doing so, we are building the foundation for motivation. We are laying out supports that students can take hold of and build momentum as they learn new concepts, no matter where they start. That's what matters here. Learning progressions are great and have been a valuable tool in my classroom, but it's the shift they've facilitated in philosophy, perspective, and environment that has truly made the difference.

HACK 3

APPROACH ASSESSMENT AS A TOOL TO BUILD CONFIDENCE

Help Students See Their Success as Motivation for the Next Challenge

Once we believe in ourselves, we can risk curiosity, wonder, spontaneous delight, or any experience that reveals the human spirit.
— E. E. CUMMINGS

THE PROBLEM:
STUDENTS FEAR THE ASSESSMENT PROCESS

Just for a second, imagine that you start class one day by saying, "Okay, students. Today's our big test day!" and a student jumps onto a chair and leads the class in applause. Even if we scaled it down from that extreme example to just having a student smile when you say the word "test," it still seems like an unimaginable scenario, which highlights one of the worst things about assessment in school.

In most schools and classrooms, the assessment process is no longer connected to supporting learning in the minds of students. Instead, it's connected to the idea of ranking and sorting. Ask any student to tell you the purpose of a quiz, and I'd be willing to bet they say, "To see if we learned what we were supposed to learn."

Nothing is wrong with that answer, but what stands out to me is what's missing. Rarely do I hear mention of future learning, of growth and potential, or of how it helps them move forward. That's partially due to how assessment is used in classrooms (as the "gotcha" moment we often feel tied to), but it's also the general culture of testing that has developed in the United States. When students think about big tests, they undoubtedly think about the big state tests. The function of these tests is to rank and sort. Either they can graduate, or they can't. Students almost never get to see any data from those tests that supports their future learning because they've often already moved to the next grade by the time the results arrive.

For students who have fragile academic confidence, a test has the potential to tell them, "You're not good enough, and you never will be." We must recognize that when we are careless in approaching grading and assessment in our classrooms, we send the message that assessments are an attack on students' academic abilities and on their very identities.

For some students, this fear of being attacked results in inaction entirely. We call these students disengaged or unmotivated because they don't even try. While this may occur for a variety of reasons, one might be that until students attempt something, they can tell themselves whatever they want about their ability to be successful. Put another way, until we have evidence that says otherwise, we have nothing to refute whatever we tell ourselves. We have students who might not know if they will be successful on an assessment, so instead of discovering that they don't know something, avoiding the assessment becomes a defense mechanism to protect their identity

> *By providing multiple opportunities to attempt to demonstrate learning, we show them there's a way to calculate their grade so it values growth and honors mistakes as vehicles for learning.*

and their confidence. When viewed this way by students, assessments aren't just the opposite of motivating; they are antithetical to the idea of success, and this closes the door to future learning.

For learning to happen, vulnerability must be present. We must be willing to confront hard truths and expose our abilities before we're even aware that we have knowledge to learn. However, we can't just tell students to be vulnerable. Vulnerability is usually built through a combination of psychological safety and confidence.

In terms of psychological safety, students must believe that the assessment isn't an attack, and they build this belief through the foundations of how we use assessments. Students must know that we use assessments to support them. By providing multiple opportunities to attempt to demonstrate learning, we show them there's a way to calculate their grade so it values growth and honors mistakes as vehicles for learning. We show this by being clear and transparent about our assessments and the essential learning they are meant to demonstrate.

As many of these background elements have been addressed in previous chapters, this chapter primarily focuses on the second element needed for people to be vulnerable: confidence. Now, this might be confusing because confidence and vulnerability might seem on opposite ends of the spectrum, but increasing research, specifically the work of Brené Brown, shows the two are closely linked.

It takes courage to be vulnerable, but courage typically only exists alongside the potential for success. While we can find many examples of courage in the face of certain defeat, these examples often reflect extreme situations where the person has a clear and powerful sense of purpose, driving them to stand tall in the face of insurmountable odds. We think of historical narratives like the Alamo, religious stories like David and Goliath, or modern-day heroes like Malala Yousafzai.

However, our students aren't in these situations, and frankly, facing down a test doesn't carry nearly enough sense of purpose for students to be courageous even when they feel like there's no way they will do well on it. Knowing this, part of our goal as educators must be to use the assessment process to build student confidence so they gain the courage to be vulnerable and, through that process, be able to make learning meaningful for themselves. If we don't, students won't feel confident in their abilities to be successful, and that lack of confidence will present itself as a lack of motivation.

Sounds easy when you say it, but what does this look like when it comes to the nuts and bolts of how we assess students in the classroom?

THE HACK:
APPROACH ASSESSMENT AS A TOOL TO BUILD CONFIDENCE

If you've never felt successful at something, how do you know it's possible? More precisely, if you haven't seen progress toward success, do you have any reason to believe that your effort is paying off or that it's even worth trying?

This is what I think about when I start planning an assessment sequence for any bit of learning I'm asking students to do. How am I building assessment sequences to help students see their success and growth so they build the confidence they need?

To explain this, I'll start by sharing what I used to do that didn't build student confidence. Let's say, for example, that I'm trying to teach students to write complete sentences, but to assess that, I'm asking students to write an essay. If the essay is the only work I'm using to assess whether a student is learning how to create complete sentences, how are students going to feel approaching that assessment?

For starters, the only evidence they have to support whether they will be successful is how they did in previous classes or the grade they got on the previous essay. This is why we so often see students get trapped in a performance loop. Students who got an F on their last essay will approach the next essay with that evidence and convince themselves success isn't on the table for them. The students with an A might find themselves on the opposite end of the spectrum, full of confidence and convinced they have nothing left to learn. At this point, the assessment process does nothing more than cement identities students have already created for themselves.

How do we shake these identities and approach the assessment process in a way that breaks this narrative for students and provides them with evidence that success is possible for them this time? The answer stems from a topic we've already talked about—learning progressions. With learning progressions, we focus on how we scaffold the learning process to make it clear and explicit for students to support them when they get stuck. However, the learning progression also helps to create an assessment sequence that we can use to help students build their confidence and gather evidence to support a narrative of success.

Here's what this could look like. Let's go back to the example we were just looking at with students learning to write complete sentences. If we were to build a learning progression around that, it could look like Image 3.1.

SKILL: I CAN WRITE COMPLETE SENTENCES.				
PHASE 1	PHASE 2	PHASE 3	PHASE 4	PHASE 5
I can define nouns, subjects, verbs, and predicates.	I can identify nouns and verbs when given sentences.	I can correct errors in end-of-sentence punctuation when given an example with errors.	I can write simple sentences and identify the subject and predicate.	I can combine simple sentences together into compound sentences.

Image 3.1: Complete sentences learning progression.

We now have a foundation for building an assessment process that scaffolds student confidence. Again, the goal is to provide students with evidence that they can be successful. If the end goal is to write a full essay with complete sentences, then this progression tells us how we can build an assessment sequence that helps provide students with evidence that shows their competence at each stage, which, as we've talked about before, engages them in a competence-confidence loop to build their ability to see success along the way.

In my classroom, I often use the term *checkpoints* when I talk about assessment with my students. I like to help them see each assessment as a stopping point to make sure they understand the basics before moving on. For our first checkpoint, I would have a digital, automatically graded assessment that checked phases one and two together. Through a series of intentionally designed multiple-choice questions, students would check to see if they know what nouns, verbs, subjects, and predicates are.

The goal here is to create an early stage of success for students, which is why I prefer to provide an automatically graded assignment for this checkpoint. When I don't have to grade it, it makes it much easier for me to allow students multiple attempts at this checkpoint. Typically, at this stage, I tell students to wait until they get above 90 percent before they move on. It is rare that students get stuck here because of the simplistic nature of the concepts at this phase, but if they do, I often leverage time outside of class to support them, whether it's during my thirty minutes of contracted time after school or a twenty-minute support period we have built into our schedule.

From there, I create a second checkpoint for students to see if they learned phase three of the learning progression. With this example, because this phase still focuses on lower levels of thinking, it's possible that I can also automate this assessment process using a digital tool.

I do want to mention that when we automate assessments, it's key that we are intentional in helping students see the questions they get wrong or right as feedback. I ask students to fill out a half-page sheet that requires minimal time and energy when they attempt a checkpoint, and it helps them reflect on the assessment and what it showed them. On this sheet, I ask the following questions:

- What questions did you get right?
- What did it show that you learned?
- What questions did you get wrong?
- What does that mean you should learn next?

The goal is to keep this simple and to focus on helping students see how the assessment connects to learning, both in what they've already done and the learning they have yet to do.

Confidence builds when students see the connection between their past success, their level of effort, and their ability to see success in the future.

When we get to phases four and five, I can assess this work through the writing we were already working on in class. Often, phases four and five are set up to allow me to assess those skills within the curriculum or whatever writing I planned, so those assessments are already built into the curriculum. The difference, though, is that now I have already scaffolded student confidence so they have evidence showing they can be successful on this assessment.

However, we have to make sure we encourage confidence through meaningful information, not just through surface-level praise. It can be so tempting to tell students, "You've got this! You're going to do great!" but there are two problems with that. The first is that we become the source of confidence-building in this situation, wherein the student relies on us as an external source of confidence. This is temporary and easily broken. Second, it doesn't connect their confidence to previous learning and effort. Confidence builds when students see the connection between their past success, their level of effort, and their ability to see success in the future. When we take out any of those three, we're left with a shaky form of confidence.

What we want to do, and the solution to the fear students have about assessments, is to find their confidence by using evidence that they can be successful by clearly sequencing assessments to build competence and confidence along the way. When we do that, students can use assessments for learning and see their value because it's not just a one-time "gotcha" moment or a tool for ranking and sorting. Rather, the sequence becomes a path, a series of stepping stones, and each one helps them find their way to the next one.

WHAT YOU CAN DO TOMORROW

While the process I just described might seem cumbersome, as if you have to create a bunch of learning progressions and assessments for it to work, that's not true. You can take smaller steps to begin shifting assessment from a fear-inducing to a confidence-building experience.

▶ **Create a checkpoint quiz.** You don't have to build a whole series of checkpoints to build students' confidence. Start small. Just make one checkpoint assessment that students take as many times as they need to until they learn it and are ready to move on. This could be a small digital assessment that's auto-graded (my recommendation, both for time but also for the immediacy of information for the student). It could be a checklist the student uses to self-assess. It could be a conversation they have with you before moving to another step.

It doesn't matter what it looks like, but it does matter what it covers. This should be an assessment that covers the basics of a concept, possibly even background info from previous years that will support the newer concept. The goal is not to make an incredibly rigorous assessment. The goal is to make an assessment that will show students they have what it takes to be successful from the get-go.

▶ **Make an assessment reflection tool.** An assessment reflection tool is exactly as it sounds: a way for students to reflect on their performance and to make meaning out of their results. The simpler, the better when it comes to these. This is a tool students should be able to pick up independently and complete. It should be a balance between helping them think deeply about their results without encountering too high of a cost-benefit gap so the energy required doesn't outweigh the benefit of the learning in the student's eyes.

Here are a few elements that I've found helpful to include:

- Have students reflect on which questions they got right and which questions they got wrong.
- Have students think about the content of each question, focusing on what concepts/skills they see most often.
- While keeping it simple, have students name the learning or the next steps they need to take because of this assessment.

The goal is to help develop the idea that assessment is not an isolated incident or a one-and-done way of ranking students. The reflection tool, when focused on future learning, helps students understand that assessments serve to help them grow.

▶ **Adapt an assessment by leveling it.** Maybe you aren't ready to dive in fully with the learning progressions discussed in the last chapter, but this could be a smaller, more assessment-focused approach to sequencing the learning. To help with this, think about the different depth-of-knowledge questions you can ask students. Could you build or rearrange questions around different depths of knowledge and then have students complete the steps in an intentional order?

Essentially, you could start with the earlier questions being somewhat simpler or more basic and then create different sections that get more complex or focus on more advanced concepts.

The benefit of this for the student is that the organization allows students to see what they've learned and what they need to learn next. When assessment scores are all lumped together, it can be hard for a student to identify their next step. When they can see that they've already been successful in some areas, it often makes them more motivated to try in the areas where they are still struggling.

A BLUEPRINT FOR FULL IMPLEMENTATION

STEP 1 STEP 2 STEP 3 STEP 4 STEP 5 STEP 6 STEP 7 STEP 8

Use a learning progression.

While it's possible to create an assessment sequence without a learning progression, I've found that by clearly articulating what the learning process might look like, I'm much more able to align my assessments with the learning I am hoping to see from students as they progress in understanding the concept.

STEP 1 **STEP 2** STEP 3 STEP 4 STEP 5 STEP 6 STEP 7 STEP 8

Build a checkpoint assessment.

I've heard them called gate quizzes, checkpoints, pit stops, and more, but the idea behind all of them is the same. How can we give students multiple opportunities to demonstrate the starting steps of a learning process? These also bring accountability for students to understand the basics before moving on. I've found the latter step to be just as important as the former.

The reason accountability early on is so important is that it ensures students don't move forward with a false sense of confidence that can be easily shattered. For example, let's say that a student never learns the difference between an independent and dependent clause. They may get by just fine writing simple sentences for a long time, but eventually, they will get stuck figuring out how to punctuate complex sentences or how to create more variety in their sentence structure. At that point, the student may not be able to pinpoint the actual issue, and as such, they will end up confused and frustrated. It's in these spots where you hear kids resign themselves to saying, "I'm not good at writing," or "I'm not good at math."

All that is to say checkpoint assessments are so valuable. When we assess with major projects or large, all-encompassing tests, these little elements often sneak by unnoticed until they become major issues later.

These checkpoints don't have to be complex or large. My goal is to keep them under ten questions that are all focused on the first one or two levels of a learning progression. I do this for two reasons. First, it ensures they have accountability to learn those background elements and encouragement to move on once they get it. Second, and just as important, these levels of questions are often manageable and can be assessed using technology.

Many people bash multiple-choice questions, and I understand where they are coming from. For far too long, we've used multiple-choice questions unproductively. I think I got through college almost entirely because I was a good test-taker. Nearly every test I took was multiple choice. However, multiple-choice is often a poor tool for assessing complex levels of thinking, and unfortunately, because of their ease of grading, they end up on summative assessments to measure the understanding of concepts that are more complex than choosing A, B, C, or D. It's either that, or we end up sticking with lower-level questions in terms of depth of knowledge because it's easier to automatically grade assessments that way.

If we use multiple-choice questions as a tool for what they were intended, though, they can be an effective part of the learning process. These checkpoints are a great opportunity to use multiple-choice questions as the tool to measure our students' understanding, basic grasp of a concept when given an example, and identification of sentence errors. This is why I use them so often in my earlier checkpoints.

When you build your checkpoint, remember that the goal is for students to take these as many times as needed, ideally with a reflection after each attempt, like the one shown earlier in the chapter.

STEP 1   STEP 2   STEP 3   STEP 4   STEP 5   STEP 6   STEP 7   STEP 8

Build an assessment reflection tool.

Because the goal is to have students attempt the checkpoint assessment in the previous step as many times as possible, it's important to add a pause-and-reflect stage before the student attempts the assessment again. If not, you may find kids just rushing through it as many times as they can, clicking randomly on answer options until they get lucky enough to get them all right. If that's how the checkpoint goes, they didn't learn anything that they'll retain.

Instead, focus on having students pause after each assessment attempt and reflect on how they did to identify the learning left to do. After all, that's the entire point of taking an assessment: to check to see what you've learned and where you need to go next. Keep these reflection tools simple.

The process I like involves two steps. First, students reflect individually on their performance. They analyze which questions they got right and which they got wrong, looking for patterns in their assessment results. The goal is to help them see what they've learned and then narrow down one or two concepts they must learn before the next time. Second, I add space under the reflection that says, "After consulting some resources, what have you learned that will prepare you for next time?" This helps narrow the gap between assessment and learning to make the information feel more immediately important for the student and to help them see that, while they may have struggled on the assessment, they still have the capacity to learn the content. Again, motivation is about helping students see a route to success.

However it looks, the goal in this step is to create a pause so students will slow down, process their results, and transform them into actionable steps.

STEP 1 STEP 2 STEP 3 STEP 4 STEP 5 STEP 6 STEP 7 STEP 8

Build a controlled assessment.

I've fallen into the same trap too many times in my career. Perhaps you can relate. The trap is to use large, time-intensive, and effort-intensive assessment methods—like a giant project, a multiple-page essay, or something of that size—and then wonder why a student didn't engage in it. Do I want students to learn to accomplish big things? Absolutely! It's one of my areas of focus with my students—time management and task management. However, if that is the only method to assess student understanding, then I'm not allowed to be surprised when a student doesn't finish the one big project and then has no evidence of their learning to provide to me.

For example, let's say I'm assessing my students' abilities to write a conclusion paragraph. Typically, I used to do this by having them write an entire essay and then assess the conclusion separately from all the other skills I'd be looking at in the essay. However, if the student doesn't complete the essay, I'm left with nothing, especially because they likely got some writing done but didn't make it to the conclusion at the end.

Another element is apparent when you put yourself in the mind of someone who struggles with the content area. If English isn't my native language or I have gaps in my learning, writing a sentence is daunting. Writing a paragraph is exhausting. Writing an entire essay? That will take a miracle of motivation, especially if I don't have evidence to tell me I can be successful at it.

What's the alternative? What if, instead of banking on the all-encompassing essay as the sole source of evidence about learning, we just had the student write a single conclusion? Couldn't we provide them with a pre-written essay or outline and then just have them write the conclusion? For starters, it gives them something to practice before the large essay. It also gives us a much simpler task to give feedback on, which saves us time in the process.

The student approaching the task of writing a conclusion isn't facing the overwhelming task of writing an essay; instead, they just have to try a conclusion. The extraneous factors that could get in the way of their ability to write a conclusion when drafting a full essay—such as not having a clear idea for the essay or struggling to write an introduction—are removed, and the student can focus their energy on the single concept at hand.

What could this look like in other content areas? Maybe in science, you're analyzing an ecosystem. Instead of saying, "If this one element changes, how does that change everything?" you could say, "If this one element changes, how will it impact this other element?" It's the same kind of thinking, but it's focused and targeted. The same goes for a social studies class. Imagine you're teaching students how to identify reliable sources. Instead of having students just hop on the internet and explore to find examples of reliable and unreliable sources, you could simply provide one article and ask students to rank how reliable it is and explain their answer.

Again, it isn't that we are never getting to the bigger, more complex, and often more authentic tasks. We're just adding a checkpoint that is more controlled to allow the student to focus on the skill at hand without too many moving parts to help them see success. We want them to experience success, build their confidence, and develop the motivation to engage in future learning.

STEP 1 STEP 2 STEP 3 STEP 4 STEP 5 STEP 6 STEP 7 STEP 8

Create a method for peer assessment.

The controlled assessment is where I see the biggest benefit in peer feedback. Because there are fewer factors at play, it's less overwhelming for the students giving the feedback. They don't feel like they have to focus on everything. They get to focus on one thing, and as a result, the feedback ends up being more detailed and specific than the feedback on larger projects.

Ideally, this process is built into the experience before the student even submits their assessment to the teacher. While we will talk much more about feedback in the next chapter, this iterative process of assessment is a great spot to integrate peer feedback, especially at this stage. My process for helping students with peer feedback involves walking through an exemplar together to look at what makes a quality response, talking through the learning progression to refresh on the learning we are focusing on, and then asking students to identify one or two specific areas they would like feedback on from their partner. Having students request specific areas for feedback is probably the biggest piece of the puzzle in terms of ensuring that this process is meaningful. Not only does it increase buy-in from the student requesting the feedback, but it also helps students who are uncomfortable critiquing or criticizing another's work to recognize that they are offering value because the feedback was requested. One of my favorite ways to help build this culture of constructive feedback is through watching "Austin's Butterfly," which shows how a student used feedback to make a drawing better and better over multiple revisions. In watching this and reflecting on it as a class, we usually come to a better understanding of why feedback matters, how to be specific and supportive with our feedback, and how to receive and use feedback well.

Some questions I use to spur reflection and feedback include: (1) Based on what your partner has asked you to look at and what you saw in their work, what's the next thing that would be most helpful for them to focus on? (2) If your partner were to revise this project, what's one thing they absolutely should not change and why? (3) If you could give two overarching comments to your partner to help take their learning and project to the next level, what would they be and why?

STEP 1 **STEP 2** **STEP 3** **STEP 4** **STEP 5** **STEP 6** **STEP 7** **STEP 8**

Create the last assessment in the series.

Now that students have done the initial checkpoint of looking at the background information and foundational concepts, and they've done the controlled assessment, it's time to think about what their large assessment will be. The goal is to either (a) ask students to connect the current content to previous content or (b) work with the content in a new or novel context. If you're lucky enough to teach at a school that allows for interdisciplinary projects, this is a great spot to bring this in.

However, this should not be an exciting project kids only get to do when they are done. When I talk about sequencing assessments, my guidance often gets misconstrued that students can only engage in rote and heavily structured activities until they get to this phase. That's not the case at all. If I'm working with students on building a fictional narrative, I don't make them wait to be creative and create their own until they've shown they know everything else first. Instead, students will start their fictional narrative at the beginning, and as they learn new steps in this assessment process, they go back to revise their narrative.

The reason I highlight this is that when we withhold creativity until the end of the process, much like it appears we are supposed to in Bloom's taxonomy, we often remove the purpose and reason to learn the content in the first place. Using the prior example, if students are already engaged in creating a narrative they care about, not only are they invested in what they're doing and motivated to engage in the activity itself, but they also feel it gives them a purpose to learn the content. If they're writing a narrative and not happy with how the story is going, they know they need to learn more. If they don't get to try their hand at the creative piece and are instead being force-fed content, they might not see the value in that information, and thus, the information isn't retained or ever learned.

So, while this step is somewhat later in the process in terms of getting it set up, you don't have to think about this final assessment as an end project. Rather, you can think about it as ongoing during the learning. It is the vehicle at the end that students use to demonstrate how it's all come together through revision and implementing their learning along the way.

STEP 1 STEP 2 STEP 3 STEP 4 STEP 5 STEP 6 STEP 7 STEP 8

Create alternative assessments.

When people ask me if I'm for or against test retakes, my answer is a shoulder shrug. I've seen schools force retakes as a mandatory policy, wherein students begin to rely on them as a crutch, not learning the material until the second, third, or maybe fourth attempt. They end up brushing off every assessment because they know they will get unlimited chances. On the other hand, I've also seen classrooms where students aren't offered an attempt to improve their performance, and it ends up stifling learning.

My answer to the question about whether retakes should be allowed is this: Students should have multiple opportunities to demonstrate their learning, even if they made mistakes on a big assessment. Notice this doesn't explicitly box anyone into retakes. As a student, sometimes I hated retakes. I didn't want to sit down and do the same thing over again, but if I were given a different way to try to learn the content again, I'd do it.

I often think about this with my students. At times, we need to go back to the same task and redo it or revise it in the pursuit of mastery, but at other times, we don't need to do that. We can try it in a different way or in a different context.

The key to making this a possibility is to have alternative assessments set up ahead of time. For example, using the previous idea of having students write a conclusion instead of just revising one, I can have a second essay or outline set up for them to use to attempt to write a conclusion again. As a bonus, having these on hand means that when a student thinks their score for a skill is too low, I can hand it to them and say, "Here's your chance to prove it." Instead of being stuck with a low score and no chance to improve, a condition that often crushes motivation, we can provide a new opportunity for growth to help ensure that motivation stays high.

You might wonder how in the world it's possible to create this many assessments. First, I've been working with mostly the same curriculum for my ninth grade English class for the past seven years, and I am still creating these alternative assessments. You feel the pressure to make it happen immediately, but if that involves taking time away from your loved ones, the activities that fill your cup, or the rest and relaxation you deserve more than you get, then please pump the brakes. There will be time. Reforming your assessment practice isn't an overnight shift.

You can also lean on the support of generative AI. What used to take hours to create an exemplar or an alternative assessment can now take mere minutes.

Additionally, to speed up this process, lean on your team. Not everybody has the privilege of a team, but with the rapid expansion of artificial intelligence, several tools can help create alternative versions of questions for you, almost like you have your own digital team of assessment-makers (be sure to always review and revise before you use the content). If you do have a team, spend time during your department meetings or professional learning communities building these assessments together. Delegate and then discuss. That process not only speeds up the time it takes to make this happen, but it also results in conversations about what good assessments look like and how to create better ones. Those conversations are invaluable.

STEP 1   STEP 2   STEP 3   STEP 4   STEP 5   STEP 6   STEP 7   STEP 8

Try it, refine it, and try it again.

At this point, I feel like I could copy and paste this at the bottom of each section, but I put it here again because I can't emphasize enough how much of a journey this truly is. I have never ended a year by saying, "Yep, this is the year that I've reached the end of my assessment journey. I've learned all there is to know about motivating students, and I have perfected my craft." Every year, I discover areas to improve and ideas to try the next year. Please know that if you try a process the first time and it bombs completely, I have been in your shoes more times than I can count. Look for your competence and use that to build confidence to take the next step. It takes practice, but it will snowball and result in incredible learning and outcomes for kids.

OVERCOMING PUSHBACK

Even if we agree that it's important to scaffold assessments and to allow space for alternative assessments to help students grow their confidence to increase their motivation, plenty of valid concerns come up, specifically when it comes to managing our time.

This seems like way too many assessments to manage. It can be overwhelming at first. When I first started approaching assessment this way, it got messy fast. The biggest area I had to change was my mindset around the assessment timeline. I was comfortable with just identifying a date for the assessment, and that's what my students did, regardless of readiness or confidence in their ability to be successful. I've shifted to planning for assessment blocks and having students attempt whatever assessment they're working on. If a student is still working on their first checkpoint quiz, they can hop on the digital assessment and take another crack at it. If a student has moved on to their controlled assessment, then that's what they're working on for that block of time. While it sounds a bit tricky to manage, I've found that when I use clear packaging and design of my learning management system, paired with intentional and repeated routines for this time, students catch on quickly.

Another reason I love this approach is that it frees me up to meet with more students. Because students aren't all following the same timeline, I can pull individual students aside after they finish one (or possibly while they're attempting one if I need to sit with them and give feedback). Not only does it provide students with the flexibility to approach assessment confidently, but it also provides me with the flexibility I need to individualize my approach to feedback and intervention with students.

However, managing the time aspect is one piece that many educators worry about, along with making the recordkeeping manageable. It has helped me to have students submit tickets every time they attempt an assessment. My ticket is simple. It asks students what assessment they did, what date they completed it, and what they learned from it. I also occasionally have a question that asks if they would like feedback and what they would like feedback on. This has helped me a ton in the age of online assignments, where sometimes the submissions get lost in the nightmare of an email inbox or go unnoticed in the learning management system. Once students have the routine down, they simply submit an assignment, grab a ticket, and put it in the bin I keep on my desk. As a bonus, it's a nice opportunity to talk with students when they come up so I can clarify their process and check in with them.

To ease your fears, kids aren't bringing millions of assignments to me each day. It feels close to what I was doing before, and honestly, with more variation around when kids submit certain assessments, it lessens my load in terms of the amount of feedback needed all at once because some students are submitting tickets for auto-graded assessments that require little work from me, while others are submitting larger assessments that need my time. However, rarely am I staring down at a stack of essays that all need feedback at the same time.

If a student is stuck on an earlier assessment, won't that hurt their motivation to try again? In short, yes. This is the trickiest spot for me when it comes to approaching assessment through a scaffolded lens that I've learned I must be hyper-vigilant about. If a student is stuck in the same place for too long, then yes, it can hurt their motivation, especially if they aren't seeing progress. For situations like this, it is important that I check in with the students who are stuck. If they have tried an assessment level for the earlier phases multiple times in a row, that's my cue that they need one-on-one time with me. I've found two different approaches to meeting with students who are stuck. The first is what I use when I notice a student is still taking an assessment and is slowly improving their score. I point out their concrete evidence of growth, since one key to helping students maintain self-efficacy is the belief that they can be successful. Along with this, I try to identify an area where they are struggling and either point them toward a resource or give them a quick tutorial on a concept. The motivation to try again will get squashed quickly if the student doesn't learn something new to get them past that hurdle when they confront it again.

The other approach I use is when a student is truly stuck, and I mean they aren't making any progress at all on the assessment. Maybe they're just getting the same score over and over, or because their motivation drops and they lose focus, they start to go backward in their performance. For these students, while I still check in with them during class, it's even more helpful to set up a tutoring time with them. If you have any sort of built-in student support time during the day, this is a great use for that time. My school has a twenty-minute period built in four days a week when students can work with us. Additionally, I have thirty minutes of contract time after school. While this meeting does help with the content aspect, the real reason is that these students who are stuck are often the ones who haven't been successful in an English class in the past, and I want dedicated time with them to help rewrite that narrative and to let them know I'm in their corner.

THE HACK IN ACTION
BY JASON AGUILAR, NINTH GRADE SCIENCE TEACHER, SUNNYSIDE, WASHINGTON

As a ninth grade integrated science teacher in Sunnyside, Washington, it's common to see students stress about school. They are coming into a new environment with lots of pressure to perform, both academically and socially, and that can be a rough transition. Watching them go through this, combined with my training through the Neural Education Institute, I realized I wanted to be a support for students, not an added burden. While so much of what we ask students to do in the classroom is connected, I noticed that one specific area seemed to produce high levels of stress: tests and quizzes.

To become more of a support for my students, I needed to reevaluate my understanding of stress in the classroom, not only its effects on academic performance but a human-centered way of looking at it. The great Maya Angelou said, "I've learned that people will forget what you said, people will forget what you did, but people will never forget how you made them feel." Those words have always struck a chord of truth inside me, and like so many excellent teaching strategies I've encountered in education, that truth has roots in how our brain functions. I am no expert in neurology, but what I learned can be summed up like this: We learn by making connections between neurons in our brain that are forming pathways. The more often we use the pathway, the stronger and easier it becomes to access. When we experience events in life that bring us happiness, a sense of belonging, accomplishment, and peace, those paths become strengthened. Being curious and solving puzzles or discovering new information also strengthens our neural pathways. The best classrooms have all of these activities happening. You know it when you see it and feel it. I might go so far as to say a teacher's ultimate goal includes this type of environment.

The beauty of witnessing our students' learning is a pursuit we strive for every day in our classrooms, but as you know, students face many obstacles. One of the largest obstacles is a natural and powerful mechanism that I was taught to call "amygdala hijack" or the "fight, flight, or freeze" response. The amygdala is a part of our brain that prepares our bodies and minds for survival in high-stress situations by making our bodies ready to take action, heightening our senses, and prepping our minds to react rather than think. While this can save you out in the world and keep an athlete from injury, amygdala hijack in a classroom could be a major obstacle for a student to overcome. In our classrooms, we ask students multiple times a day, in different subject areas, to problem solve, analyze, create, and produce evidence of their thinking, but when their brains are in amygdala hijack, all of that takes a back seat and their choices become narrowed to reactive, avoidant, and disengaged responses. Any perceived threat could trigger this response in a person. Public speaking is probably the most famous example of this. The brain tells you the situation is a threat, and your cognitive processes slow to a crawl, you freeze, or you bail altogether.

In time, I understood that I should be more aware of the world others live in and that I should consider their perspective, if I were to be of service. When students enter our classrooms, they invent a world with their peers and me, and it is my job to create safety and opportunities for learning. I cannot change the world they bring, nor can I change the experiences in their lives that shaped them to this point, but I can develop tools in the classroom that limit stress and increase safety and security. When they feel safe and secure, they can be open to learning in powerful ways.

While I wanted the process of assessment to be a tool for reflection and to support student learning, whenever students heard the word "test" or "quiz," I could see their stress levels rise. I remembered back to when I was a student, and I felt like tests simply measured how much of the teacher's words I remembered. In my classroom, I wanted that to be different. I wanted assessments to help students see what they had inside their own heads and feel confident about that. This caused me to start thinking about how I could use assessments as tools for reflection that build student confidence and help them see what they have to offer.

One of the biggest ways I was intentional about how I changed my assessments to be supportive instead of stressful was in how I approached my final exam for the course. Instead of making it a one-shot attempt, a "gotcha" moment, I changed it to allow students to have three attempts at it over multiple days. This way, they could use it as an actual support for learning. They would attempt it one day, have time to reflect and process it, and then attempt to improve it again later. This helped students see that they did know a lot of the content, and they could use that as background knowledge to correct any misconceptions and improve their learning for the next attempt.

I didn't make this change in isolation, though. In conjunction with intentionality around notetaking and their science notebooks, students were allowed to use those as supports during the assessment. This meant I did have to change the final a little bit. While about 40 percent of it was based on the content, which they could find in their notebooks, the other 60 percent was focused on helping them learn to use that content and apply it in new and novel ways. They could use their notebooks to give them a boost of confidence and help alleviate some stress while still pushing their level of thinking deeper.

The other piece I changed that helped students approach assessments in general, but particularly the final, with confidence was that I allowed them to help me come up with questions for the test. I got this idea from some advice about parenting. Essentially, the advice was that if you want kids to eat their veggies, let them be involved in the cooking. They're much more likely to be willing to try something if they're involved in the process. This worked well when I brought it into my classroom. When kids were involved in developing questions for the test, they were much more likely to approach the assessment with the understanding that they had some of the knowledge they needed to be successful.

As a result of all this, the difference in how students approach assessments in my room is noticeable. Where before, the stress was palpable, now, it could take a back seat so their brains could do their best work. I would be lying if I said that this produced immediate academic gains. It is still a process I'm working on, and like any change, it takes time to find its groove. Even without seeing those academic gains, this is a change I will never go back on. Students now see my support for them in how I design my assessment process, and they know I'm on their side.

Students are often afraid of assessment in the classroom. They've been conditioned over and over that the purpose of assessment is to rank and sort and to tell them if they're good enough or not. My hope is that I didn't treat that reality flippantly in this chapter. It is very real and very powerful for students. We can't flip a switch and make them realize assessment is a good thing. It takes time and practice. Students will make progress toward seeing assessment as valuable, then struggle once and revert to their old mindset about it. One bad result could crush their motivation to be successful.

However, helping students see assessment as valuable is one of the most important ways we can prepare them for the future, not just in terms of maintaining their motivation by understanding that failure is a powerful part of the learning process but also because shifting their mindset about this can have positive long-term benefits. A student who fears assessment grows up to be a person who fears feedback in a variety of contexts, a person who would rather cover up their shortcomings and stagnate than embrace the vulnerable process of identifying areas for growth and then improving. A student who fears assessment ends up being the opposite of a lifelong learner.

However, look out into the real world, and you will rarely find someone afraid to authentically assess their abilities. A kid learning to skate will practice ollieing repeatedly. A kid learning to play guitar will stumble over chords time and again. A kid learning how to play a video game will die over and over on a hard level, and yet every time they respawn, they're willing to try again.

All these examples reinforce that kids aren't inherently afraid to be assessed. The process of being assessed is as natural as breathing. A baby wobbles on its feet and falls many times, and at no point thinks, "Oh, this is so embarrassing. Those people are watching me. I probably should stop trying." It's when we get older that assessment becomes scary because failure is stigmatized, and in most academic contexts, it is permanently held against us.

Once we've been conditioned by the education system, peers, and parents that failure is bad, assessment becomes an incredibly vulnerable act. We are looking in a mirror of academic ability and facing some hard truths, knowing that those results will be interpreted and viewed by others. That's not comfortable, so I view it as one of the most valuable aspects of learning that I can help students accept. It's our job to do whatever we can in the classroom to make assessment more than just a rank-and-sort activity. Our job is to show students that when you fall short, you get right back up and try again, and eventually, through that effort, success will be within your reach.

When we think about designing assessments and assessment systems in our classroom, this thought must be at the forefront of our minds. We must know that assessment is all about helping students learn from their mistakes and that we are working with students who have been conditioned to fear mistakes. Mistakes, when penalized through grades or when made in environments that seem to stigmatize them, are often a motivation-killer. As such, we can build a system that scaffolds confidence in students by allowing them to approach it in manageable chunks and struggle as much as they need to without being penalized at each step along the way. That's no easy task for us, but sequencing assessments intentionally is one way we can begin that journey toward transforming assessments into learning experiences that truly build motivation and confidence in our classrooms.

HACK 4

CONNECT EFFORT, SUCCESS, AND NEXT STEPS THROUGH FEEDBACK

Create Feedback Systems
That Focus Students on the Future

The key to learning is feedback.
It is nearly impossible to learn anything without it.
— STEVEN D. LEVITT

THE PROBLEM:
INEFFECTIVE FEEDBACK DECREASES MOTIVATION

It's estimated that one-third of feedback interventions decrease performance and drop student motivation (Kluger and DeNisi 1996).

One-third. Let's talk about what this really means. This means that when teachers take home a pile of papers and spend hours providing meticulous comments to help students, one-third of those hours were not helping students, so they were wasted time that could have been spent with loved ones or engaging in hobbies.

Early in my career, I often felt feedback was futile. I'd leave comment after comment highlighting areas for growth, only to see those same areas for growth in the next writing from the same student. And the next. And the next.

Yet, I'd end up back at it again when the next piece of writing rolled around, often sitting at my kitchen table during unpaid time, doing what I thought I was supposed to do. I was doing the same thing over and over, expecting different results. I don't even understand how I was still surprised when the feedback was disregarded. I knew that's what would happen. I would groan, "Why isn't this working?!" and then do the exact same thing again.

So, it was in this state that I finally decided I needed to change. It was the act of confronting actual data that proved my processes weren't benefiting the learning. I committed in that moment to get rid of the one-third of the comments that were wasting my time and lowering my students' motivation to learn.

I thought I would start by digging in and researching what "bad" feedback is and what "good" feedback looks like. Some of my research blew my mind. For example, you may be familiar with the "compliment sandwich," a technique where you provide a positive piece of feedback, then some criticism, and then another positive piece of feedback. I don't believe I was ever taught this explicitly. It's just so engrained in our culture of feedback that I inherently picked it up and started using it.

Then I found an article that looked at the impact of "compliment sandwiches." Granted, it was from the business world and not specifically for an educational context, but the points still rang true. First, a compliment sandwich downplays the value of constructive criticism. By buffering the criticism with something positive, we are communicating that criticism is negative and must be balanced by something positive. A negative association with constructive criticism is not what I want to instill in my students.

Second, it begins to build negative associations with positive feedback. If every time you give me a piece of positive feedback, you immediately follow it up with criticism, then I'm going to fear positive feedback as an omen of bad feedback on the way. Along with this, it results in feelings of mistrust and inauthenticity between the deliverer and receiver. I was unsure where this came from at first, but then I thought about how often that second bit of positive feedback ended up being a bit of a stretch. The second positive part of the sandwich might as well have been me writing, "Good font choice in Times New Roman. Very classy." It was often devoid of substance, and students are good at picking up on inauthenticity.

One final bit of the study that caught my eye was this: the compliment sandwich is primarily used to benefit the deliverer, not the receiver. Nobody likes being the bearer of what could be considered bad news. As such, we bolster the bad news with bits of praise so we can walk away feeling like the good guy when we've really added potentially harmful or irrelevant bits of information that make it less likely students will remember what they need to work on (Von Bergen, Bressler, and Campbell 2014).

The point of this is simple: We must question our assumptions about feedback and what makes it effective. To begin, we can look at what makes feedback ineffective, at best, and harmful, at worst. As I dug into this, I was afraid I'd find guidance that would require me to spend more time leaving feedback because my assumption was that better feedback was synonymous with more feedback, or rather, more detailed feedback. As an English teacher who routinely brought home stacks of papers at this point in my career, that was off the table. Fortunately, what I found instead is that most of the research supported spending less time leaving feedback, but I had to find out some ways to leverage technology to make it all efficient (my favorite thing) and yet more effective.

Early in my research, I learned that I was giving way too much feedback.

Early in my research, I learned that I was giving *way* too much feedback. I was the teacher who made papers bleed red. Every misplaced comma, every missed period, every misspelled word—I had to mark them all. I felt like if I didn't, the students wouldn't know they had learning to do. At times, I would hand back papers with, honestly, nearly a hundred marks on them. At the time, I thought I was being helpful, but in retrospect, I know I did harm to students, and it's tough to grapple with that sometimes.

What I've since learned is that the optimal amount of feedback to provide to students is the equivalent of three comments on an essay (Nicol and Macfarlane-Dick 2007).

Three.

That's it.

This is because our brains are efficient, and part of this efficiency means we have to quickly make decisions about which information is relevant and which is not. When we receive a wave of new information, our brains can essentially shut down, which people familiar with the brain will know as cognitive overload. When we hit this state of cognitive overload, our amygdala kicks in as a reactive measure. This is why, when you see students receive lots of feedback, not even necessarily negative feedback, they seem to shut down. They may get quiet or defensive. They may deflect or distract from it. They are trying to avoid dealing with it because it's just too much to handle at once. It's frustrating to see them just check the paper and move along quickly, but what we have to be mindful of is that this might be their amygdala taking over with a fight, flight, or freeze reaction.

We don't have enough room in our working memory to process all that information at once. As great as our brains are, they are fickle. Overloading them with too much information is a surefire way to prevent learning and to kill motivation.

When this study mentions that we need only three comments per piece of writing, they add one more crucial piece of information. The full statement says, "... three well-thought-out feedback comments per essay was the optimum if the expectation was that **students would act on these comments**" (Nicol and Macfarlane-Dick 2007).

That part of the statement, "if the expectation was that students would act on these comments," is the key. We can give students all the feedback we want, but if we surpass the three comments, we can't expect them to act on all of it, or any of it.

So, now we know that ineffective feedback is feedback that is overwhelming or too numerous to be useful. What else?

Well, vague feedback is also harmful. There are a couple of elements to this. The first piece is praise. One of the biggest shifts as a result of Carol Dweck's work on growth mindset, especially highlighted in her book *Mindset*, is the idea that vague praise focused on ability is actually harmful to someone's view of themselves as a learner.

While we use phrases like "Great job!" or "You're so good at this!" in attempting to build student confidence, we can be undermining it in the process. It's important to note that a good grade at the top of a paper can fall into this category, too. Think about it this way: If you were to make a gift for someone, and when you brought it to them, all they said was, "This is incredible! You are such a talented artist!" you might feel good. However, what if that person then said, "Can you make me another one just as good?" What has happened now is that expectations have been set without any communication of what specifically resulted in the work being of such high quality. Now, you must attempt to engage in that process again, knowing that the bar is set high, but you don't have any clarity about what you need to do again or even what you could do to improve. You're trying to recreate some form of success that you may not fully understand.

This is what Dweck says begins to create fixed mindsets, and this is where the harm starts to occur. You think, "I'm a good artist because someone liked what I did," but then the following question inevitably pops up: "What if someone doesn't like what I do?" What this feedback has done is link your value and success with nothing more than the product you create without providing specifics about the actions that led to the success.

Not only will this kind of feedback raise the anxiety and stress levels of the person attempting to recreate their performance, but it also can increase the fragility of their confidence. In a scenario where a student might already not feel confident in their ability, this type of feedback can often lead to the complete disengagement we see when students receive a negative result in their next attempt. Their fragile identity that began developing with their last success has been demolished. They may feel as though they are playing a game where they don't know the rules, and when that happens, nobody wants to play for long.

The last element of ineffective feedback that we'll cover in this section is feedback that is not relevant to future content. Now, this covers a couple of different applications. First, we can be more mindful of the amount of time it takes us to provide feedback to students. As an English teacher, I find this part the hardest. When I collect 120 pieces of writing all at once from students, it's hard for me to get feedback to students in a timely manner. The problem is that if I take too long to leave feedback and move on to something new in the meantime, I've lost the window for the feedback to be useful. I've been guilty before of returning feedback that's too late to be used, and what I have to realize is that leaving feedback without providing an opportunity to *use* that feedback to improve is nothing more than pointing out a flaw. If students don't have the opportunity to use the feedback, then don't leave it.

Second, curricula often aren't the best at spiraling, or revisiting previous standards and content. In situations where the curriculum doesn't spiral, it can diminish the usefulness of feedback. Again, our brains are good at getting rid of useless information, and if I receive feedback that I can't use immediately or in the near future, my brain will decide pretty quickly that it's not relevant information. If we want students to utilize feedback, we have to make sure they have a relevant application for that feedback and an opportunity to grow and improve as a result.

While many other elements of feedback make it less effective, these are the big ones: it's an overwhelming amount for our brains, it's not clear enough to help us know what to learn moving forward, it's too connected with grades or praise to engage students in a growth mindset, and it's not given within a relevant context for it to be utilized.

At this point, you may be wondering if I'm the most negative person in the world or if I'm going to talk about solutions and the positive side of feedback. I promise I am, and here we go.

THE HACK:
CONNECT EFFORT, SUCCESS, AND NEXT STEPS THROUGH FEEDBACK

Imagine for a second that you're a crime scene investigator. When you arrive at a crime scene, another investigator tells you they've already jotted down lots of notes for you to read and try to find patterns and meaning. When you ask to see the notes, they point to the crime scene, which is littered with sticky notes spread out all over with individual observations written on each one. How quickly do you think you'd be able to make meaning out of all that?

How do I ensure students can easily access all their previous feedback and make meaning out of it?

It may seem like a ridiculous scenario, but we do the same thing with students and feedback throughout the term. We commonly leave isolated comments on individual assignments that a student has to dig through to find, and then we wonder why they didn't use them. This was the thought that led me to consider feedback portfolios. I realized I was scattering information all over the place for my students, and in that process, the meaning was lost. Students couldn't see trends and patterns. If I left a comment on one assignment and the same comment on the next, it was difficult for my students to even notice that. It was easy for them to disregard the feedback because it was out of sight and out of mind. My question then was, "How do I ensure students can easily access all their previous feedback and make meaning out of it?"

The resulting idea was a feedback portfolio. It's nothing complicated at all, simply a place for students to record their feedback and possibly categorize it by learning outcome or function. Image 4.1 shows an example of one of my favorite templates to use.

LINK TO YOUR WORK	DESCRIPTION OF TASK	GLOWS (SUCCESSES)	GROWS (NEXT STEPS)

Image 4.1: Writer's portfolio.

That's it. That's all it is. I've seen this done in several ways, including a cool slide deck portfolio where students display their work with feedback next to it, and a flap on student folders where teachers put feedback portfolios so the students see them every time they open the folder.

How they look doesn't matter as much as the fact that they exist. Think about what this opens in terms of opportunities for learning. First, simply the act of transcribing, summarizing, or categorizing the feedback means students interact with it more than just acknowledging some comments on a paper and moving on. This act of rewriting the feedback can help signal to their brain that this is information worth holding onto.

Writing it down somewhere also has an added benefit. If their memory decides to get rid of this information, it's not buried in an obscure assignment they will never look at again. We've taken those isolated bits of information and put them where the student can easily access them.

Both of those aspects of feedback portfolios are important, and even more important is what they allow students to notice. When the bits of feedback were spread out all over, students couldn't see any trends. As a result, they couldn't see growth. With the template, students can often see skills move from their "grows" column, which identifies areas they need to work on, into their "glows" column, which is where they are celebrating their success.

This can be huge for some students. It reinforces the idea that they struggled with a concept, but through effort and learning, they grew in that area and can now celebrate growth. I occasionally have students do reflection activities specifically focused on this growth with their feedback portfolios because I want to make sure students reflect on their progress and tie it to their effort. When students struggle with this, or just struggle to accurately record feedback in general, I make sure to spend individual time with them so they can see this growth. The prompt is usually, "What is one area where you are seeing growth, and what actions did you take to make that happen?" Linking growth to efforts and actions is one of the most powerful activities we can take to support kids in developing their academic confidence, and for this to happen, we must first create an environment where they can see that growth. As a bonus, if we do this in a space devoid of grades, that makes it even more powerful.

While this step is crucial, it is nothing more than a foundation for meaningful feedback. Yes, students need a place to record and compile their feedback, but they also need meaningful feedback to put in there. So, this then is our question: "What is meaningful feedback?" We've looked at the inverse of this, and now let's focus on the positive. What do these comments look like? If I'm not marking individual corrections, what am I doing?

For me, the goal is to leave comments that identify trends. These trends are often what indicate learning needs instead of just errors. For example, if I'm reading a student's piece of writing, I'm not going to mark every single time they put a comma where they should have put a period. Instead, I'm going to leave a single comment at the top of their piece that identifies comma splices as an area for future learning.

The term that sticks with me when I read feedback research is the term "advisement" to describe the ideal bit of feedback. When you think about advisement or someone's role as an advisor, their job is to take in a bunch of information, process it, and then give pointers on what the person could do. That's my best description of meaningful feedback. Students may not have the content knowledge or expertise in the content area to take all that information and make meaning of it. If we are just marking the mistakes and asking them to figure out what to learn, they may not be able to. Our job, then, as people well-versed in our content, is to process the information and tease out the bit of learning that will be most valuable to the students.

I started adding one note somewhere on the student's work. It was a simple question: "What are you working on that I could help you with?"

Again, we are only providing a few comments to students, though. We can't put ten things on there that they need to learn and expect students to engage with all of them. It's more likely that sharing too much feedback means that they interact with none of it.

Another key element of feedback is that it must be goal-oriented. I sometimes catch myself leaving feedback that's totally irrelevant to the goals we've been working toward. For feedback to matter, it must be connected to a goal that matters. The entire point of feedback is to provide guidance on how to close the gap between where the student is at and their goal. If they have no goal, they have no use for feedback. If they don't care about the goal, they have no interest in the feedback.

It's that last point, students being interested in the goal, that changed how I started the feedback process. I started adding one note somewhere on the student's work. It was a simple question: "What are you working on that I could help you with?" That's it, and that change made a huge difference in how students perceived feedback. Feedback wasn't only a set of messages I was force-feeding into their brains, whether they liked it or not. It wasn't an attack. It was seeking a response to a request. If, at the top of their draft, the student asked for help on a specific skill, I was now offering a resource they wanted. The goal wasn't solely teacher-driven; it was student-driven because they were asking for help. This simple shift changes their willingness to be receptive to feedback.

To review, we now have two major elements of effective feedback. First, it has to be focused on trends that identify the next steps in the learning. To do this, we need to be selective, curating information until we've pinpointed a couple of the most important elements to focus on. Second, feedback has to be focused on clear goals. While it's a good thing to focus it on goals we've established for the class, focusing on goals students are identifying for themselves will go a long way in opening the door for that feedback to be received well.

I want to focus on one final element of effective feedback, and that's the relevance of the feedback. For feedback to be useful, the student has to have an opportunity to use it. This is a big reason why, in Hack 1 regarding setting up your recordkeeping system, I emphasized the need for space for multiple attempts to demonstrate proficiency. Students who have several chances have a reason to engage in feedback. Students who don't have opportunities for multiple attempts are receiving a dose of criticism with no ability to do anything about it.

This gets a bit into the retake/revision debate again. Often, grading reforms are introduced with the idea that students must be allowed to retake or revise any work they do. I understand the thinking behind it, especially in systems where assignment scores are averaged over time to determine a final grade. Students who struggle on an assessment without the ability to improve are penalized in the long term, even if they show growth after that assessment. In this case, yes, it's important that we allow students the chance to remedy this by retaking or revising an assessment.

Instead, if we are using a summative evaluation model and looking at the student's scores over time to then evaluate their final score for the essential learning, then we have other options. The phrase I prefer to use instead of "revisions and retakes" is that students are afforded multiple and varied opportunities to demonstrate their learning. This means that we might have five different assessments, activities, or projects they can use as evidence of learning. In this scenario, no, a retake on one of those assessments isn't necessary because, as long as the student grows and improves, that score won't be held against them in the long term.

No matter how you approach it, it's essential that when students receive feedback, they are afforded an opportunity to use it. This should be intentional, which means we need to dedicate class time to students reviewing the feedback so they can put it into practice. My favorite way to do this is twofold. First, as soon as possible after the student has turned in an assignment, I offer feedback. Then, we take time to review it and record it in our feedback portfolios. If students have resources to watch or read, I make sure to dedicate time for students to explore them and record their learning. Then, prior to their next attempt to demonstrate that skill again, we revisit the feedback so they remember what they learned and what they want to try.

The key is that students must know there's a purpose to examining and interacting with the feedback. Feedback without the opportunity to grow and improve as a result of receiving it is nothing more than a slap in the face, and when students who are already struggling to feel confident in this area receive that slap in the face, it will hurt their motivation to engage in the future.

So, we just covered three elements of meaningful feedback. One of the most helpful actions I took in this regard was to plan out my feedback timeline. I did so by asking three questions: (1) When will the student provide me with evidence for this goal? (2) When will I provide them feedback? (3) Most importantly, when will the student use this feedback? Knowing that for myself allowed me to communicate this with students. I was able to say, "Hey, you got some feedback from me. On your next assignment, you're going to be able to use this to try to grow a bit." It might sound simple, but explicitly naming when the feedback would be used helped students to see the relevance of it. While they probably could guess that it would be used in the future, making that concrete for them helped it feel more tangibly useful.

While meaningful feedback could be the subject of an entire book, these three elements, if intentionally incorporated into all the feedback we give, will make a huge difference in our students' willingness to engage in the feedback and in its application in subsequent attempts.

As we near the end of this Hack, have you noticed how many times I've referenced the teachers giving feedback and how few times I've mentioned students *providing* feedback, either for themselves or a peer? This is one of the most difficult exchanges to cultivate in a classroom culture, but when we utilize it well, it can be so valuable. In studies, student self-assessment (when paired with a clear rubric and exemplars that are analyzed collaboratively) has shown to be just as accurate as teacher-assessed scores. As such, when we set up students for success, self-assessment can be a tool that saves time in providing feedback for students. When they engage in self-assessment well, they can often answer this question: "Based on what you saw when you evaluated your own work, what's the next thing you want to learn?"

That right there is the goal of feedback: students can explain what they need to learn next. I have found myself in a place of arrogance, assuming I'm the only one who can provide the type of feedback for my students that ends up creating this level of success. While it is true that students who don't have sufficient content or background knowledge (and as a result, often lack the level of confidence needed to critique their own learning) struggle to know where to start in providing feedback for themselves, most of our students can do it when they are set up for success with clear rubrics and exemplars.

While much of the space was dedicated to talking about feedback through the lens of a teacher, the content being discussed applies directly to student self-assessment and peer assessment as well. For example, in peer-feedback scenarios, a huge benefit is in having each student identify what they would like feedback on before the group dives in. While it requires a bit of vulnerability up front that has to be cultivated through building a classroom culture of trust, once a student names what they would like support with, it completely changes the dynamic of that group. Then, their peers aren't as afraid to give constructive criticism that could be misconstrued as mean or hurtful because their peer has openly requested feedback on that skill. In addition, it gives a sense of psychological safety for the writer or owner of the work because they aren't waiting to hear about issues they didn't realize they needed help with. Rather, they've engaged in a process of reflection around their work, identified an area of need, and understood that the team will focus specifically on that area.

Similarly, if we want peer feedback to be useful, we must provide an application of that feedback in the near future. My favorite way to track this is to create a simple chart with three columns labeled (1) The sentence receiving feedback, (2) Feedback from peers, and (3) Revised sentence.

This simple chart helps translate peer feedback into actionable and immediate guidance, and recording it like this allows the student to reflect on how that small interaction, that little bit of feedback, can lead to improvement if they utilize it.

WHAT **YOU** CAN DO TOMORROW

A nice component of making changes to how you provide feedback to students and how students provide feedback to each other is that you can make a number of small changes now that will have a fairly large impact on the effectiveness of the feedback itself.

▶ **Build a feedback portfolio that works for you and your students in your context and content area.** Not every feedback portfolio needs to look the same. I've seen portfolios where each piece of essential learning for the unit has its own spot for students to record feedback. This has the added benefit of having students categorize their feedback, forcing them to think more about the feedback as they engage in this process. You may want to provide a physical feedback portfolio as opposed to a digital one, especially if you don't have daily access to technology. The goal is for students to see them regularly, so access is key. Keep in mind that feedback doesn't just mean written comments from the teacher. Missing a question on a math test is feedback. Building a tower that falls apart is feedback. When these activities happen, the feedback portfolio can be a vehicle for students to pause and reflect on what they need to learn next as indicated by this feedback.

▶ **Learn to leverage technology to make your feedback faster and multi-modal.** I've spent a few years of my career as an instructional technology coach and have provided workshops at schools and conferences about educational technology and meaningful integration, and I can say without a doubt that one of the best ways to incorporate technology is in our feedback processes. For starters, screen recording makes it easier than ever to provide video feedback to students. With a screencast, I can focus on a couple of issues and talk the student through them in detail, highlighting certain passages, making changes, and explaining them. The added benefit is that the student then takes the feedback from one medium and transfers it to another as they record it in the feedback portfolio. This adds a little more work on their brain to help convince them the feedback is worth hanging onto.

Similar to video feedback is audio feedback. My tool of choice is Mote, which allows you to embed audio comments directly into Google Drive files. While this has a multitude of applications (i.e., explaining directions, pronouncing words in readings), my favorite use is in leaving feedback. While it's not a full video, students still get to hear my voice, and it humanizes the feedback more than a written comment.

The third way I lean on technology to enhance feedback, and this one is a favorite, is using a text expander. Say, for example, that you are constantly writing a note to students about their use of fragments in their writing. I can go into my text expander

and write out a detailed comment that explains what fragments are, why they're bad, and how to avoid them, and then I
decide on a shortcut I can use to insert the entire comment. For
this example, maybe my code is *!fra*. When I type in those four
keystrokes, and entire paragraph pops up, explaining everything thoroughly, and I've added that comment in a mere frac-
tion of the time it would have taken me to type the whole thing
out. It's key to mention that I don't add this whole comment
every time I see a fragment. Instead, I leave a single comment
somewhere on the piece that identifies this as a trend. Limiting
the number of comments in this way helps students avoid that
cognitive overload scenario where they begin to shut down.

Additionally, most text expanders have the capability of insert-
ing hyperlinks into these comments. Now, in addition to the
detailed explanation, I can link to resources that further the
student's learning. Just think about the possibilities this opens!
With just a few keystrokes, I can provide completely differentiated resources to every student in my room if needed. This is
the kind of stuff I used to dream about before I started integrating technology into my feedback.

▶ **Develop a routine for self-assessment and peer
evaluation.** Early in my career, I struggled with using self-
assessment and peer evaluations well. Sadly, I blamed the
students when it didn't go well. You'd think, by this point,
I would have learned my lesson that, while it's always
partially on students to engage in productive behavior,
I have a role in setting them up for success. First, students
must frequently engage in both self-assessment and peer
feedback before they start to do it well. It's like anything
else we're trying to learn. When we begin, we struggle. Once
we do it multiple times, we improve. We should treat any

sort of group work in the same way. Certain skills absolutely need to be developed for this to be a productive time.

A second element that applies to both self-assessment and peer evaluation is to pause and examine some exemplars, talking about what we notice as effective or valuable. That gives us a goal to aim for and one that we can compare and contrast with our own or others' work. Having this in their minds as they examine others' work helps students pinpoint specifics for their feedback. Additionally, for peer review, psychological safety must be present for students to be willing to engage with each other in critiquing and providing feedback on each other's work. *The Culture Code*, a book by Daniel Coyle, talks about why some groups thrive while others struggle and that one of the biggest factors in determining the effectiveness of groups is the existence of psychological safety.

As such, before I have students work together in groups, my goal (and I know this sounds funny) is to have them laugh together. Laughter is a major social bonding tool, so when forming groups, it's common for me to start them off with a quick game (even a round of Uno or some Apples to Apples) or a challenge (a breakout activity like an escape room of sorts) to help build this psychological safety with each other. Along these same lines, I try to keep groups consistent for multiple rounds of peer feedback. Consistency allows those relationships to develop, and it means the next time we have the opportunity for peer feedback, we aren't starting from scratch. Rarely, I will adjust the groups if a need arises due to behavior or other factors, but my goal is to keep them as consistent as possible.

The next element of my routine, specifically with peer evaluation, is to have students identify specific types of feedback they want out of the peer evaluation time. We start by referencing the learning progressions and the feedback portfolios so students can home in on what feedback and support they need. Just like with teacher feedback, having students identify goals they want feedback on helps them see the feedback as valuable, and in this context, it also helps the rest of the group see the need to provide meaningful feedback. When students are given a peer review sheet with pre-set questions for them to take notes on, it can be hard to see how you are offering value. It feels like you're just doing busywork, which is why students might treat the peer review time with disregard. When someone has specifically asked us for help, our reaction is different than filling out a pre-made worksheet.

Finally, I have learned to rely heavily on timers, especially in peer review. My goal is to eventually wean us off timers so the process can be more organic, but I have found that the use of timers ensures that everyone gets a turn and pushes students to go beyond surface-level discussions. Without the timers, I would often see people zoom through it without providing much substance. When I add in a timed element, I set the expectation that each person gets feedback the whole time. Groups often hit a wall early, but with some prompting, they begin to go into more detail with their feedback, and that is often where the substantive and meaningful feedback information is hiding.

Another valuable tip is to build in a revision time immediately after the peer assessment. This gives an immediate application for the feedback. In addition, ask students to identify what they changed as a result of the peer feedback. This may be a comment left on a digital document, or it could be an exit ticket they hand to me as they leave class.

As a bonus, whether in self-assessment or peer evaluations, I often highlight my favorite sentence and have students reflect individually or discuss with their teams why it might have been so good. Especially when they are new to these processes, many students will have negative feelings about showing others their work, again going back to the fragility of their academic identity. Many students are not at a place where their confidence in their ability is high enough to allow them to be receptive to criticism and critique. By highlighting the best but not telling them why, the individuals and teams spend time essentially building up each other's confidence by talking through all the reasons why the sentence (or passage, sometimes) was my favorite. This almost always ends up having a positive impact on student motivation because not only do they get to feel successful, but that feeling ends up spreading through the classroom as all students get to talk about their own success and the success of others.

A BLUEPRINT FOR FULL IMPLEMENTATION

STEP 1   STEP 2   STEP 3   STEP 4   STEP 5

Build your feedback portfolios.

This helps lay the foundation for your students to begin using feedback meaningfully. Fortunately, this step doesn't take long. It's simply a matter of deciding how you want students to organize their feedback. Do you want the feedback categorized by essential learning? Do you want the feedback organized by unit? By glows and grows? If you just want to dip your toes into the feedback pool, it doesn't even have to be organized. It can just be a space for the assignment name and a space for the feedback.

As with all the insights in this book and any area of teaching, don't focus on making it perfect right away. Make it workable and then improve as you go. I promise you that no one else cares whether it's perfect. A disorganized, colorless feedback portfolio that students are using is a lot more effective than the almost perfect one you're still making that students haven't even seen yet.

| STEP 1 | **STEP 2** | STEP 3 | STEP 4 | STEP 5 |

Map out your feedback timeline for the unit.

We are often good at mapping out our curriculum and our assessment timeline, too. We don't plan out our feedback timeline, however, and this may result in forgetting to leave feedback, providing feedback too late, or not being intentional with class time around feedback. Feedback should be a part of the lesson plan, not just a part of what we do outside of class time. Here are the three big pieces for me when planning:

- *When and how am I gathering specific evidence that I (or other students) will use to provide feedback?* When I plan the assessments with the feedback I want to provide as my guiding element, I find that I'm more intentional with how I develop the assessment. The nice thing about this is that it can save time. If I'm only focusing on sentence structure, I know not to leave feedback on all the other aspects I could comment on. Knowing this ahead of time allows me to be more targeted and intentional with how I develop the assessment.

- *How and when will I give students feedback?* This was never an area I planned early in my career. I would just fit feedback in when I had time, and what ended up happening was that I would put it off or get sidetracked until the feedback was too late. I've since shifted to using my calendar and lesson plans to identify when I'm going to leave feedback. I block off my planning period three days in a row (and cross my fingers I don't get the dreaded call to go cover a colleague's class) so that I know that's what I'm doing with my time.

  In school, we don't treat feedback with as much value as we should. It's often a process we forget about or put off because other aspects have more immediate consequences if they aren't finished. If lessons aren't made, thirty students suddenly have nothing to do. If emails aren't responded to, administrators and secretaries get annoyed with us. Sadly, if feedback isn't provided, the impact is not as noticeable. We can't let feedback get pushed to the side and devalued in our rooms. While its impact is not felt as quickly as other tasks we do, it is one of the most valuable actions we can take in our classroom. Meaningful feedback is how students truly learn and grow.

- *How and when will students use the feedback?* Just like we planned time to provide the feedback, we can also be mindful of planning the time that students will use the feedback. This is time for them to record it in their feedback portfolios, to explore the resources that will help them move in the right direction, and to process it together in groups. We make time for what we value in the classroom, and students notice what gets time and what doesn't. If students don't see feedback as valuable, I can often look back and notice that I hadn't given it much time during class. One of my favorite routines around feedback time is to summarize key points from the feedback in our feedback portfolios. Then, students pinpoint one concept they want to learn about from the feedback. They might have resources from me, or they might have to find the resources on their own. Either way, they have time to explore and learn. Finally, I have them record in their portfolios and share with a partner or two what they learned that they plan to use the next time.

Does this take up more time than I used to spend on feedback? Sure. I have to adjust some of my lesson plans and activities so we have enough time for feedback. Nonetheless, it is definitely more important to me that students get good feedback that makes a difference than it is for me to deliver a full lesson or add in an additional practice set of problems.

If we want kids to value feedback, we need to show them that we value it, too. While it might be concerning at first to trade what we consider instructional time with time for students to process feedback, the resulting growth and development in our students, when we're intentional about providing time for processing feedback, will make it more than worth it.

STEP 1   STEP 2   STEP 3   STEP 4   STEP 5

Build support elements for your feedback (such as HyperRubrics and text expander comments).

If you are planning to incorporate digital elements into your feedback processes, this will take time to set up in advance. For me, I almost always focus on creating my text expander comments first. It takes a bit to type out the comment I want to show up when I use the shortcut and to find the resources I want to include in the comment as a link. However, when I think about the amount of time it saves me while I'm leaving feedback (especially if you count the multiple years that you can use these comments, even if you tweak them a little), the net effect is a massive reduction in total time spent on feedback.

The idea is to create a bank of resources you can pull from as needed to turn your feedback into advisement. This doesn't have to be fancy at all. You could have a digital document with links to videos about specific concepts that you copy and paste into your feedback. Google Classroom has a comment bank feature built directly into it, and many other learning management systems have similar features. As you plan for this, think about your answers to two questions: (1) How can I provide resources for students to keep their focus looking forward at what they can learn next? (2) How can I do this in the most efficient way possible? Again, if feedback is an overwhelming process that takes you away from the other aspects of teaching that you love, then you will be less likely to do it. Just as we want to provide feedback that matches the way students' brains work so they use it, we also want to think about how to hack our own brain so we are more likely to provide feedback. If we know a task will be tedious, time-intensive, and ineffective, we will find every excuse possible to avoid doing it. This is that cost-benefit ratio at work again. However, if we can set ourselves up so that our process works quickly and allows us to provide meaningful feedback that impacts future learning, then the cost-benefit ratio on our end will balance out to ensure we are likely to engage in the work, too.

Establish feedback routines.

Students aren't used to engaging with feedback. Sadly, many students are conditioned to ignore feedback in pursuit of the almighty grade. Simply expecting that they will be ready and willing to jump into processing and meaningfully working with feedback may lead to hair-pulling and undue stress.

To avoid this, before you even begin providing feedback to your students, create routines that will support their engagement in the feedback. The first step is to help them acknowledge the value of feedback. At the beginning of the year, I show the video of "Austin's Butterfly," demonstrating how a student goes from being a novice at drawing a butterfly to drawing a beautiful butterfly. Even though this video is geared toward younger students, it still opens up a good conversation with my ninth grade students. The reason for the improved butterfly? Austin got feedback and used it along the way to improve his skills. Though this process may not officially be part of the routine we'll use for feedback, it helps to establish an important mindset around feedback that will support our work with it throughout the rest of the year.

When I begin working with students around the routine of feedback, one of my first steps is to have them do some sort of small demonstration of their learning (for me, it's often just writing a paragraph). At the bottom of it, I will ask them to identify what they would like feedback on. I am intentional about asking them this question their first time because I want them to, from the beginning, see feedback as an intentional process designed to support them with where they want to grow.

Once they've finished the draft and identified the area in which they would like feedback, I gather that from them. Then, I'll provide them with feedback only. No grades, marks, or rubrics. This first time around, it is solely narrative feedback. We'll record that feedback in the feedback portfolio, typically in a guided fashion, as it's the first time we've used it.

Then, I will ask students to revise their work and resubmit it, making sure I'm dedicating sufficient class time to do this. I often give them extra time and am almost theatrical in how much I explain why they are getting this time and how I know this time will deepen their learning and help them produce higher quality work.

I often use a phrase I learned from *The Culture Code*: "I'm giving you these comments because I have high expectations for you, and I know you can reach them." The researchers found that using that phrase has a huge positive impact on how frequently people use the feedback. The goal here is that (a) I'm helping students get comfortable with the routines we will use, and (b) I'm helping them understand the "why" behind the feedback and how it can be useful for them.

Once they've revised it and resubmitted it, I will then provide another round of feedback. You might be feeling like this seems like a bunch of time and energy to provide two rounds of feedback on the same small item. The honest answer is that it is a bit of extra time compared to what I used to spend, but I try to drive home the importance and value of feedback early on. To do this, it takes me a little extra time. In subsequent pieces, I often only leave feedback during one round of submissions, either in the early drafting stage or at the end of a final draft, to set them up for the next piece we'll write.

Finally, and this is the part of establishing a routine that I've found to be most important in the later success of feedback and the students' perspectives of it—we record the feedback for this round of the drafts in the feedback portfolio. It doesn't happen for every student, but many students can see how their use of the previous feedback resulted in greater success in this round. That's the key I try to help them see as I establish the routines. Yes, I want them to be comfortable with the process and able to access the correct materials quickly and independently, and even more than that, I want them to see the reason for the processes and routines altogether.

STEP 1 **STEP 2** **STEP 3** **STEP 4** **STEP 5**

Gather feedback from students.

This could be said for the implementation in every chapter, but I saved it specifically for this one because I've found that gathering feedback from students about the feedback I'm providing helps me to refine what will be the best use of my time. I've had classes that loved video feedback and classes that hated it. I've had classes ask for more time in conferences with me and classes that have asked for more time meeting with peers.

I won't pretend to be able to tell you which approach will work best with your students because every year, I change my approach for my new batch of students. We must remember that despite all the theories and best practices, when it comes down to it, we are working with a unique mix of ever-changing students every year. If we want to show students that we value learning, we must be willing to be a learner ourselves. Stopping to listen to our students and showing them we are willing to change are the best ways we can show our love for learning.

OVERCOMING PUSHBACK

Many people have negative associations with feedback, whether giving or receiving it. Either it feels like an enormous burden from the teacher's side that hasn't paid off in terms of learning, or it's been a negative experience from the students' side that has turned off many of them to the value of feedback. The following are common concerns about feedback and how to respond.

Even with all of this, some students just don't care about feedback. Sometimes feedback may not be well received in the moment, and we can't despair at that because for every student who ignores the feedback, others are thankful for it and use it well. In these moments when you notice your feedback isn't effective with a certain student, look around at the others. You can typically find countless examples of feedback success. It seems we don't allow ourselves the chance to see it most of the time.

Also, this doesn't mean we should give up on the student who's not using the feedback well. When I sit down with that student and have a conversation, I hear most often that the student doubts their own ability to be successful. Maybe I left feedback that seemed like I was setting the bar too high, and we need to step back and break it down into more manageable steps, or maybe I need to provide an alternate explanation and give the student a few words of encouragement that highlight previous successes. Sometimes, this conversation has nothing to do with the feedback at all, but the student needs someone to check in with them and see how they're doing. It's often the latter conversations that end up producing benefits down the road. It might not change the use of the feedback in the present, but when the student knows we trust and respect them, they will likely be more willing to engage in the feedback later because they know we are sincere in why we are offering the feedback. (For more about why students quit and how to re-engage them, see the book *Quit Point* by Adam Chamberlin and Svetoslav Matejic.)

No matter what, though, I still ensure that every student records their feedback in their portfolio. I often see a lot of eye-rolling and groaning early on from students who don't want to do it, but I still encourage them to go through the process of recording it because, eventually, they get to see more and more of their struggles become successes. It's not foolproof and doesn't always happen, but once students get to see their success and are able to link it to their use of feedback, they will be more willing to engage with feedback in the future.

This seems like it takes up a ton more time to leave feedback in this way. At first, it does. That's the truth, and it's just like anything else we change. It's new and weird at first. It feels awkward, and we might be clumsy and slow with it. Does that mean the adjustment itself is bad or that the initial results should determine whether the change is a value-added element? Not at all. The same goes for changing feedback practices. Especially as you start to set up comment banks and create HyperRubrics, you may feel as if you are spinning your wheels. You'll want to jump right in and start providing feedback. Even after you've set things up, you might feel like the process of identifying trends and providing advisement takes you longer to figure out than simply identifying the mistakes. However, and I cross my heart on this, my feedback now takes me about half the time it used to take, and I see much better results. More students utilize the feedback. More students understand the value of feedback, and then our peer review sessions are much more focused and supportive.

The question comes down to this: Would you rather spend an hour doing an activity that would have little effect, or spend ninety minutes doing an activity that will make a difference in student learning? At first, yes, it will take a bit longer, but after a while, not only will you get faster at providing feedback, but you will also see more value in the time you spend giving feedback. The effort you put in becomes exponential in the long run, and isn't that what we all want to feel about feedback? That it's not an overwhelming burden but results in student growth?

The final piece that has saved me time is to provide feedback to students in the moment. When we're working on projects or pieces of writing, I'll ask students to have their feedback portfolios out as I go around the classroom. I'll pop in to chat with a student, provide some feedback and direction, ask them to record it, and then move to the next student. This way, I can provide feedback during class time without taking up any extra time at all.

My kids only care about an assignment if they know it's graded. Will students do the work if they only get feedback on it? This question really asks if students will be interested in learning or only in the rewards because it's how they've been conditioned. It's a completely rational question, backed by experiences of assigning work that isn't graded, only to have students not engage or take it seriously. That experience happened for many of us, and sadly, it often put a sour taste in our mouths for prioritizing feedback over the stick-and-carrot approach of grades.

First, attempting to change an element without shifting the culture won't result in success. If we have not done the work to de-emphasize grades through our practices, conversations with students, and policies, then the abrupt shift away from leaning on grades to simply relying on feedback will confuse students. When they've been repeatedly told that they have to get good grades and "To get your grade up, you need to do more assignments," they will associate value with points. Before you start using learning experiences solely for feedback and not for points, hold important conversations with your students about this.

Second, you don't have to get rid of the grade right now or altogether. We talked earlier about how using grades in conjunction with feedback often results in students not using the feedback, so the goal here is that if a grade is to appear, it doesn't happen until after the feedback is given and engaged with. Ideally, the goal is to get to a point when students understand the value so they are willing to engage in the work without a grade, but sometimes it can be helpful to simply delay the grade.

THE HACK IN ACTION
BY TONI STEPHENS, ENGLISH EDUCATOR, ATLANTA, GEORGIA

Our district required teachers to display the data from the classroom in a visible way, have students understand that data, and be able to assess their learning. The problem was that in English, you measure both quantitative and qualitative work. Also, making data meaningful for over a hundred students was time-consuming and laborious. Therefore, I designed a system in my ninth grade English course that would capture feedback, allow students to see their progress, and measure that progress as a class without extending my own responsibilities.

After the initial diagnostic test, I put the students' results into folders and then created a chart that measured the scores they received on each standard. I gave them personalized feedback, and I took an entire class period to explain the chart and their folders. They were given stickers in green, yellow, and red.

The stickers represented if they met the standard (green), were approaching the standard (yellow), and if they needed improvement (red). Students then placed a corresponding sticker for each standard based on their test results. They were able to immediately articulate the standards that they did very well on and the areas they needed to improve on during the school year. Thus, they were able to write tangible and obtainable SMART goals from their own data. They wrote this information in their folders and reflected on their goals by writing their observations.

Next, I took the standards chart and made it larger for each class. I had two ICT classes, two honors classes, and three on-level English courses. However, I listed them only by section and coded their progress with the same measurements as for each individual student. From here, students could see their progress measured against my other classes. When I say it got competitive—it got very competitive. During the year, students in on-level classes would note when they exceeded a standard over my honors classes, and students could see their progress over the entire class.

We took the time each month (or at the summative assessments) to update these folders and the data wall. Students would get their folders and update their standards chart, and then we would meet individually so I could give them feedback. When it came time to meet with students, we had specific and detailed conversations. I allowed students to tell me where they were individually and where they stood against their peers as a class. Many students were able to express that they felt they were behind or explain concepts they felt were difficult based on the data. We could also dissect the data together, and I could show them why some data may have been skewed or what happened with a particular exam. For example, a question may not have made sense, and all the students got it incorrect, or we may have changed a question midday if we thought it should be worded differently.

Finally, students thrived with this information. Several of my on-level students used the data to request English honors course recommendations for the next year, stating that they maintained or exceeded the same progress as those courses. Also, students with IEPs and 504s had detailed data to measure their progress. Students could see if they met their SMART goals and had a visual overview of the course. They were excited to look at the chart to see if it moved from red to green. Those who didn't see this progression were still successful in understanding their needs and where they had room for improvement. For those students who did not pass the course or received low scores, the data showed the gaps and effort over the unit or entire class.

This method made my work as a teacher much more fun, and it helped students to be a part of the process instead of just taking a test, getting feedback, and moving on. Students had a part in their learning. The data helped drive instruction and made it truly personalized learning. The feedback I gave them on summative assessments and essays made sense, as they could visualize it with the color-coded stickers, and they left the course with a portfolio that showed their learning over the year. I was able to remediate where needed, and I had a clear guide as to what we needed to study for the end-of-course, high-stakes exam. I ended the year with an over 90 percent pass rate and a 55 percent growth rate on the end-of-course test, and I know for sure that this feedback system, among other things, played a significant role.

Feedback is the classroom teacher's conundrum. On the one hand, it is a time-intensive process that sometimes feels ineffective. On the other hand, feedback can be the spark that makes learning happen for a student. The key is to think about feedback in its broadest sense. Feedback is simply information that tells us where we're at in reference to a goal. When we view it this way, it opens up a world of possibilities for how we provide feedback to students.

As we wrap up this section, remember that we wield great power with how we respond to student work. Purely negative information will likely end up harming student motivation and their willingness to engage again. False or vague positive praise will result in increased anxiety for students and could foster a fixed mindset based on their perception of the value of their abilities. When students find themselves in a fixed mindset, that can hinder motivation, as it can manifest in their thoughts, such as, "Well, the teacher told me I'm good at it, so what else do I have to learn?"

The goal isn't necessarily to avoid negative feedback or to not give positive feedback. The goal is to provide information that points students in a direction where they know their next step in learning. When we view feedback in this way, we can avoid the trap of thinking criticism is negative and praise is positive. Instead, we can focus on whether the feedback motivates students to learn more. If it doesn't, it's not effective feedback.

The goal, then, should be advisement. We should be focusing on using the information students provide us, analyzing it, and then pointing them in a useful direction. That's effective feedback. Sometimes, we make it more complicated than it needs to be. At its core, feedback is about helping students understand what direction would be most useful. To do this, we need to listen carefully to what they are telling us, respond thoughtfully to identify the meaning we see in the trends, and then help students see how, with effort, they can move along the path to success with any goal set ahead of them.

If we can get to a spot where we can provide feedback centered on those core principles, we will engage in meaningful feedback.

Fewer wasted nights at the kitchen table, writing comments no one will see. Less being frustrated at seeing the same mistakes over and over again, despite the time you spent providing feedback. Lowering the one-third of the time we spend providing feedback that doesn't move anything forward and instead moves students backward in terms of progress and motivation.

If we can shift our feedback to being forward-focused, students will be motivated to use it because it is applicable. If we can focus our feedback on comments that provide resources for learning, students will be motivated to use it because the learning is readily available. When we think about feedback, we must think about how it is connected to the motivation of those receiving the feedback.

HACK 5

USE ASSESSMENT DATA TO INFORM MEANINGFUL OWNERSHIP OF LEARNING

Support Students in Understanding What, How, and Why to Learn

Control leads to compliance; autonomy leads to engagement.
— DANIEL PINK

THE PROBLEM:
STUDENTS ARE DEPRIVED OF THE
AUTONOMY NEEDED FOR TRUE MOTIVATION

Ask most students if school is a place where they experience autonomy, defined as having control over what they do, and I'd be willing to put a lot of money down that I know the answer almost every student would give. For most students, the answer is a clear no. At a core level, for eight hours a day, students are told where to go, what they need to do, whether or not they can use the bathroom, and even when they can talk. Couple this with the fact that one of the most important requirements for a person to truly feel deep motivation is autonomy, and it shouldn't be a surprise that sometimes we see minimal effort and engagement from our students.

As an adult with what should be a fully formed brain to make rational, wise decisions, I would react the same way as my students. When we have zero control over what we do, it's rare that we have any interest in doing it.

Going back to the three key elements of intrinsic motivation—autonomy, mastery, and purpose—we'll focus on the first one in this chapter. Autonomy is all about the freedom and the ability to control what we do. It's the ability to pursue what we're interested in and to choose the processes we take.

As we begin exploring what ownership looks like and how to better leverage it in our classrooms, I want to take a minute to pause and mention the reality that schools are not inherently places where students experience full autonomy. When you put two thousand students in a school, it would be chaos if students were able to do anything they wanted at any time.

So, the goal can't necessarily be full autonomy for students. The factors that limit the autonomy students have in schools are outside of our control and would take years and years to change. Do we need to take a hard look at how schools are designed, the sizes we allow schools to be, and how we set up schedules and classes? Without a doubt—yes, but for the sake of this book, my scope is narrower.

What I'm focused on with autonomy is the balance of decision-making between students and teachers. Specifically, these are some of the important decisions we need to be thinking about:

1. Who makes the decisions about *what* the students need to learn?
2. Who makes the decisions about *how* they will learn?
3. Who makes the decisions about *if* they have learned it?

As we get going, I want to make it clear that I'm not saying the goal is to walk into our classrooms every day and look at each student and say, "Whatever you want to do, do it." Having said that, some days I do start class by saying, "Figure out what you need to learn today and learn it." That's how I test how well I'm doing in providing meaningful feedback and information to my students, how well I'm doing in creating a culture of learning, and how well I'm doing in supporting my students' abilities to become independent learners. However, this doesn't happen every day.

When a student doesn't learn the content and we forge ahead anyway, what are we telling students?

With all of that said, the goal also isn't the assembly line version of schooling that happens in almost every school I've ever visited, where no matter how well a student has learned a topic or skill, we test and move on. Think about the impact that has on students and their motivation to learn. When a student doesn't learn the content and we forge ahead anyway, what are we telling students? What message are they hearing? That it's not important if they learned the material? That we don't *believe* they can learn the material? That we're more concerned with the rest of the class than we are with them?

Granted, that would never be the intent of our actions, but our intent doesn't change the fact that the student is still receiving those messages. This approach to schooling is the result of significant increases in the number of students we educate, making it necessary to run an education system this way, yet we still have the ability to change this in our classrooms.

We can look around our rooms and find places to dial up the autonomy for our kids so they see themselves as active agents in their own education. When we run schools in ways that prioritize systems over students, we end up creating schools where students don't feel like they have a say in their learning. This results in schools filled with students who aren't interested in learning. It's not for them, and it's not about them. Why should they care?

Think about yourself. Just like my example of mowing the lawn as a child from earlier in the book, what are the areas of your life where your autonomy has been taken away? How do you feel about those activities? You may be thinking that there are still areas as an adult where you don't experience autonomy, but you still must do certain things. We pay taxes, even though that's not exactly a feeling of autonomy. We do the dishes, but that doesn't feel like autonomy.

Autonomy doesn't mean anarchy, and autonomy isn't reflected in every action you take in life. The same goes for the classroom. There will still be activities that students don't necessarily choose to do. The goal is that we've intentionally incorporated enough autonomy so the students are more willing to engage in the moments when they don't have autonomy because they are already invested in the learning.

THE HACK:
USE ASSESSMENT DATA TO INFORM
MEANINGFUL OWNERSHIP OF LEARNING

I want to highlight a word in the heading of this Hack. That word is "meaningful" ownership of learning. I was good at providing ownership to students early in my career, or at least I thought I was. Most of the time, my idea of ownership was equivalent to throwing someone in the deep end and hoping it turned out well. It was messy, chaotic, and unstructured. Sometimes, that is how learning functions, but when it is the structure used to run a class, it doesn't go very well.

I knew deep down that I wanted students to be able to have ownership and autonomy in my room, but I just didn't know how to approach it. I ended up needing to break it into a few different areas. As such, I view ownership as separate in the following two areas to help me target my efforts.

1. **Ownership in the process of learning:** I focus on thinking about how I can share power with students in identifying what they need to learn and how they need to learn it. The two subcategories are:

   - **Ownership of the progress of their learning:** In this area, I ask myself if students are able to say, "I need more time," and have their request be honored. Conversely, if they've demonstrated they're ready to move on, can they do that?
   - **Ownership of the concepts they are learning:** In this area, I ask myself if students are able to identify the concepts they need to work on, and if they have an opportunity to do so.

2. **Ownership in the outcome of learning:** This area centers on student grades. My goal, as someone who works in a school that requires a final grade like most other schools in the US, is that the process of determining a final grade is transparent and collaborative and allows the student to be active and empowered to have a say in their final grade. I've found that most of the harm of grading comes from the "smoke and mirrors" feeling that students have around it. They feel powerless to impact their grade, and that's never a spot we want students to be in.

When I started teaching, many people told me ownership was the goal, but rarely did anyone show me what it looked like. This entire chapter boils down to one key concept: **learning to have conversations with students around their performance to help guide them in owning their next steps.**

My first approach to student conferencing was simply to explain to them why their grade was the way it was. It was truly just a grading conference, but I quickly found that this approach wasn't having the desired effect of motivating students in their learning. This is why I refer to them as "learning conferences" and not "grading conferences" now. As much as possible, I have moved away from the practice of discussing grades during these conferences.

Now, students show me their work, talk about their highs and lows (areas where they are seeing success and areas where they're stuck), and we talk about their next steps. I don't want to make it sound too simple because there are many key elements around these conversations that make them productive, but I know that when I first started exploring the concept of student conferences, they seemed so much more complicated in my head than they needed to be. In essence, you just need the following elements:

1. **A method of sharing student data with them, organized by learning outcomes.** Fortunately, two pieces that we've already talked about lend themselves nicely to this. The first is a learning progression. The second is the feedback portfolios. Both of these, in combination with some reports of students' data over time, when done through the appropriate lens of clarifying the connection between effort and growth and discussing support moving forward, can have positive impacts in boosting motivation after these conferences.

2. **A self-reflection tool for students.** This step is a huge piece of making conferences efficient. When you have thirty-plus students in the room, you need to budget time for independent or group work to make space for it, but just as important, you need to leverage reflection tools ahead of time so students already know what they need to talk about and we can hit the ground running.

3. **A conversation guide or template.** When I started learning conferences, I would sit down and look at pieces of their work, talk about what I was seeing, and ask a few questions, but it felt like we were meandering through it all. I've switched to a simple structure that I keep consistent every

time. First, we have a personal check-in. I always start with this as a subtle way to remind students that they are what matters most, not the work. Second, I ask, "Where have you seen growth since we last talked?" followed by, "Where do you feel like you've gotten stuck since we last talked?" Finally, I ask, "What is the most important thing for you to do next?"

4. **A follow-up planning tool.** If they don't walk away with a tangible reminder of what they will do next, it's unlikely that the learning conference will make much of an impact on the student's learning. As a bonus, you can use this follow-up tool when the student begins the reflection for their next learning conference to see if they've grown since then.

That's it. Create data that both you and the student can use, give students time to reflect, have a structured conversation, and then make a plan. It seems simple, and it does eventually feel that way, too (although probably not at first; it takes a minute to get these figured out, so don't lose heart if your first few rounds don't feel as productive as you'd like).

"Assessment is how we learn to listen deeply to students."

The heart of all this, and why it matters, was captured beautifully by a fellow teacher who said these words that have stuck with me ever since: "Assessment is how we learn to listen deeply to students."

This is where the true value of these learning conferences lies. For a more concrete example from my content area, let's say I know a student who is struggling with writing complete sentences. If the only tools I'm using are the student's writing and some quizzes I've given, then yes, I'm listening, but I'm doing so incompletely. I might be able to leave feedback for them that encourages them to investigate what a fragment is and be more careful about using periods in their writing, but am I sure that I understand the issue and have provided a solution that will help them? In these conferences, I can really understand what is most valuable for the student to focus on next, and I can provide them with opportunities to pursue it.

Going back to the opening of this section, this is why the word "meaningful" is so important when we talk about ownership. For ownership to be meaningful, it must result in greater future independence, deeper conceptual understanding, and an increase in the student's confidence in their ability to be successful.

This is a tall order, especially when we limit ourselves to an incomplete tool set. In my assessment practice, I've begun to use the analogy that my assessments are the bricks, but the conversations are the mortar that holds everything together. If I try to build a structure using only bricks, it will stand for a while on its own, but eventually, an outside force will cause it to crumble. If I'm trying to build a strong understanding of a student's learning, I need those conversations to fill in the gaps and give me a more complete picture.

The way I approach these conversations varies slightly, as I've learned there are three different types of conversations I have with students, depending on where we are in the learning. Those three types of conversations are mid-unit conference, end-of-unit conference, and end-of-term conference. Part of the reason why I've shifted to these three types of conversations is because they help me to be more efficient in how I approach discussions about student progress.

Here is what each type of conversation usually focuses on.

Mid-Unit Conference: For this, I ask students to bring me the best sample of their work with some reflection around why they are proud of it, and then to bring me the most important question they need to ask about their learning. The first piece, highlighting their best part, is huge in helping build their motivation. Prior to this, I provided written or recorded (video or audio) feedback on individual pieces of their writing, and it was in that feedback that I would highlight a win for them. While this helped, having students identify their own wins not only engages them in metacognition around thinking what quality looks like, but it also changes the dynamic of who is in control of telling them they are successful.

However, while the first piece of the conversation helps build their confidence, it's the second piece that typically results in future learning. Now, you'll notice that I only ask students to bring me their most important question. This is for two reasons, the first of which is time. If a student shows up with ten different questions, that will take up a good chunk of the class period, and I won't be able to talk to all the students. More important, though, is the fact that having students come with lots of questions means they won't be able to make progress on any of them. If I want students to act on the information from the conference, that information needs to be as limited as possible.

The other benefit of having students prioritize their questions and challenges is that it helps them process the information more deeply. When we reflect on our learning, it's easy to identify multiple areas we are confused about. Often, students will highlight specific mistakes and errors they see on a test, in their writing, or with a project. If we talk about the mistakes, they may get them fixed, but the more important conversation is about the trend those mistakes identify.

Sometimes, learning is stifled by the inability to ask the right question, so as much as these mid-unit conferences are about me providing feedback, encouragement, and support to the student, they are also about training students to ask better questions about their own learning. Motivation often grows only when we feel like we can make progress independently. Learning to ask the right question is a huge part of that.

End-of-Unit Conference: For this conference, I tend to zoom out to look at the bigger picture with students. The two questions I focus on are: (1) Where have you seen growth in your learning? and (2) Where do you feel like you're currently at with each skill? The learning progressions are a valuable tool here.

Again, just as in having students highlight what they did well on as an individual task in the mid-unit conference, this has them focus on their growth to celebrate it. The tricky part is that when I provide students with quantitative data, they often don't reflect and instead point to the skill that has the numbers going up. As such, I don't use quantitative data for this step of the conference. Typically, students use their feedback portfolios to support this step instead.

The second element of these conferences is helping students to think critically about where they are in their learning for each of the skills we've worked on in the unit. This piece is where it's crucial for students to understand that the score on the page is an approximation, and they have the right to show me evidence that proves they deserve a different score. Without this understanding, this step often carries little value. When I began these conferences, I would typically say, "Okay, tell me where you think you are on the learning progression." Students would look at their progress reports, check their most recent scores, and then use those to point at whatever stage in the learning progression was reflected in the numbers on their progress reports. This resulted in shallow conversations that didn't impact the course of their learning at all.

Two major practices have helped these conversations be more productive and useful. First, I've implemented a student work portfolio that accompanies these conversations. This is separate from the feedback portfolio and is incredibly simple. It's a slide deck with a slide for each concept we're learning. On each slide is space for students to record what they've learned (we often take notes physically and then transfer the key points into the portfolio) and space for students to place an example of their best work that connects to the skill. We use the portfolio as the center of our discussion, talking about what they have learned about the skill instead of just what scores they've gotten. Second, my goal is, eventually, to not even have the progress report out for these conversations. I may bring them out to discuss specifics and talk about growth, but when I start with the progress report, the conversation ends up feeling stifled.

As I walk away from these end-of-unit conferences, my goal is to end up with an agreed-upon level for each concept we focused on in that unit and as needed, a plan for the student to continue working on the concepts they need to work on. This isn't limited to academic concepts. These end-of-unit conferences are times when I discuss academic behaviors most pointedly with students. I try to identify one specific behavior for students to improve and give a tip for what they could do better.

End-of-Term Conference: This conference has been the trickiest for me to figure out how to focus on the learning. Because of the nature of how our schools are set up, I still have to end up giving each student a grade. There's no way around that, so it's during these end-of-term conferences that we finalize their grade for the term. This idea of collaboratively determining a grade can make certain stakeholders uncomfortable (administrators and parents, especially), so it's important to communicate openly with all parties and clarify that this is still a process based on data and student performance with clear guidelines for how it takes place.

When I initially started holding these conferences, I would spend almost the entire conference talking about what final score they had earned for each skill and what grade that would result in. It felt very "box-checky" and not productive at all.

I soon realized that the entire discussion focused on their past to determine their grades, when really, most of that was already determined. During the end-of-unit conferences, we typically would agree on a cumulative score for each skill, so rehashing all that during the end-of-term conference didn't feel useful. In my mind, I was trying to overexplain the scores so students would feel like their grades were fair, but it still ended up feeling like I was telling them what we both already knew.

Instead, talking about the final grade is now one of the fastest parts of this conference. I essentially say, "Here's what we've already discussed and agreed upon, and this is where your grade currently stands." While that may sound rushed and a little impersonal, it's the follow-up questions that bring out the important stuff. I typically ask, "What are the things I'm not seeing about your learning and behavior in your grade right now that should be celebrated?" Then, I follow up with, "Based on your feedback and reflection, what are some goals you want to set for yourself next term?"

The goal of these conferences used to be exclusively focused on the final grade. While I do want to make sure students understand their final grade and feel like it is fair based on their performance that term, I learned that the more I focused on the grade, the less value students got out of the conference. At the end of the year, this was sometimes the last one-on-one conversation I would get to have with students. The last topic I want to talk with them about is grades. Instead, we talk about celebrations and goals. We focus on their future, not exclusively their past, because the goal is, although this academic year is ending, to lay the foundation of motivation for the next year by helping them see what they accomplished this year in their learning and identify achievable goals for the next year to keep the snowball of motivation rolling.

WHAT YOU CAN DO TOMORROW

Student conferencing can feel daunting to get into, especially when you think about managing a classroom and the time element you must set aside to make it happen. While I won't lie and say it's an easy adjustment, I can tell you that eventually, it feels more manageable, and the payoff is worth it. Here are useful first steps you can take to get you prepped for these conferences.

▶ **Help build student stamina with independent or group work.** This is a crucial step. Students are often uncomfortable and unpracticed with the idea of working completely independent of a teacher, whether that's on their own or in groups, and staying focused. My wife is an elementary teacher, and she talks to me a lot about helping students build up their reading stamina by slowly increasing the amount of time they spend during independent reading and having explicit conversations about reading stamina and focus. In the age of constant distraction, the ability to focus on a project for long periods of time is waning.

Ensure that you have a good routine around cell phones in the classroom. I have gotten to the stage of having a phone check-in in my room, where each student has a numbered spot where they place their phone. I'm not saying that's the route everyone has to take, but if you want the time to be productive while you're focusing one-on-one with students, you have to figure out a good routine that is supported by administration and aligned to building practices to ensure students aren't staring at their phones while you're focused on another student.

Second, and this one's more fun, help students practice focusing on what they need to accomplish. I've found a couple of ways to be helpful with this. The first is to simply have open and clear conversations with students about what helps them focus and what doesn't. My favorite way to approach this is to have fun with it by starting with this question: "If we were completely unfocused as a class, what would we see and hear?" It starts the conversation with a lighthearted, fun approach, and it helps students identify what to avoid. From there, we talk about how we can prevent those distractions. However, I have found that ending there often has students still focusing on not doing the wrong thing, but it doesn't support them in doing the right thing. I try to follow up by asking, "What are some things that you know help you focus?" Students usually share ideas like timers, lowering the lights, and working by themselves. I use this whole-class discussion to make a list of both the good and the bad and then post it in the room for students to see as a reminder. We then slowly practice building our focus stamina during the year. I'll start with five minutes and have them practice focusing on an assignment, a choice reading, or a group prompt, and then we'll reflect briefly afterward. Then we move to six minutes and seven and so on and so forth. This has helped me move from being frustrated that they can't focus to feeling like we're making progress.

▶ **Practice micro-conferences.** The first time I did student conferences, I felt like they were incredibly awkward. I didn't know how to ask the right questions, and students weren't sure how to reflect and respond in the moment. To help with this, I started trying to be intentional with my check-ins. I practiced asking students to reflect on their work and learning in short bursts. I found the questions that worked and the prompts that pushed reflection. It almost seems silly when I write it out now, but these small moments of practicing student conferences helped me develop my confidence in creating conversations that support learning. As a bonus, it helped students feel more comfortable engaging in that process, so when it came time for the actual conference, they were already a little used to it.

▶ **Create short reflection activities for students.** Just as I was uncomfortable and unpracticed with student conferences, many students feel the same about reflection. We often approach reflection at a surface level in the classroom and in a way that doesn't impact much. For example, I was guilty of frequently using the "thumbs up if you get it, thumbs down if you don't" early in my career. Now, I'm not saying that's bad, but it doesn't require much thinking and reflecting, and it usually doesn't change anything. Students end up developing a relationship with reflection where it isn't very valued.

As such, a great first step is to simply develop short reflection activities that ask students to dive deeply into their work to think about their learning. My favorite way to do this is simple and uses the same template. Say that we are working on four different concepts in a unit. At the beginning of class, I ask them to use some sort of evidence of learning to help them decide which topic they need to focus on most. This might mean they are looking through their feedback portfolios, test results, or pieces of writing. It's helpful to pause here and have students practice developing a key question to help guide their learning, as discussed earlier in the chapter. Once they've identified which area of their learning they need to focus on, then they get time to pursue learning that area at a deeper level. Sometimes, this means I have a resource with links to help them learn about each concept, but other times, it may be time for them to explore resources that they find as they try to come up with an answer to their question.

However it happens, the goal is to get students comfortable with the idea that meaningful reflection can lead to future learning. If they don't believe that, or if they don't believe that you value that, then it's much more difficult to make learning conferences valuable.

▶ **Practice chunking independent work time with your curriculum.** I know one of the hardest parts of thinking about conferencing with students is figuring out how to fit it into our busy curriculum. If I can give you any encouragement here, for the past seven years of my career, I've worked in a school that requires me to be within five days of the curriculum with all seven other teachers in my ninth grade English team, and I've been able to fit student conferences in without falling behind my team. Now, that isn't the ideal scenario, but I mention it because I want you to know that even with a strict timeline, you can still make conferencing work.

One key to being able to make it work is to figure out how to chunk time when you don't need to be hands-on with your students. This might be independent or group work time. This might be times focused on consumption (watching a flipped lesson or reading a book) or on creation (making a poster with a group or writing an essay). Whatever it looks like, the key is to find a way to chunk your schedule so it gives you the time you need to sit down with students individually.

I prefer to chunk this work time into longer periods over a few days, but I've also seen people chunk shorter times and do them over a longer stretch of days. I typically need about three days with fifty minutes of my sixty-three-minute classes to sit down with all my students and have meaningful conversations.

I know someone who creates a similar plan but instead will take a full week and split the classes in half, using thirty minutes a day to talk with students. There isn't a right or wrong way to approach this.

Look at your next week and practice identifying the spaces where you could rearrange your plans to give yourself a few days in a row with decent blocks of time to run learning conferences. The ability to practice planning these types of lessons without the stress of actually running the learning conferences will help you get comfortable with the setup before adding the layer of management that conferences require.

A BLUEPRINT FOR FULL IMPLEMENTATION

STEP 1   **STEP 2**   **STEP 3**   **STEP 4**   **STEP 5**

Identify where you need to create space for conferences in your curriculum.

This is often the biggest barrier to learning conferences, so it's helpful to tackle this first. I like to hold them about every two weeks, and that means for every ten days of class, I'm using about two or three classes for these conferences. If that feels like too much for you right now, do what works for you. Maybe you aim to have conferences every three weeks. Maybe just at the end of a unit.

Whatever it is, create a plan for when you could fit in your conferences. If I plan for about four minutes per student, it usually is a good amount of time for us to have the discussion we need to have.

If you're struggling to figure out when to hold your conferences, think about how you can start off a unit. I often aim to have a hands-on, high-engagement introduction to the unit to expose them to the new concepts or content with some flipped lessons to build background knowledge about what we're learning. This typically frees me up at the beginning of a new unit to be able to launch lessons and then take the rest of the class to meet with students. One mistake I made at the beginning of my journey was that I would have my end-of-unit conferences with students during the end-of-unit assessment. While there are ways it could work, we didn't have the information we needed from the final assessment to have a good conversation about their learning.

Remember that you will need to plan some time before conferences to help students engage in reflection and analyze their work and learning to make sure they are coming to conferences prepared. This step is crucial in making sure students are already thinking about their learning before they even arrive at the table for their conference.

STEP 1   **STEP 2**   STEP 3   STEP 4   STEP 5

Develop a way to communicate data to students.

You may be thinking, "Isn't that what the online grade book is for?" Well, yes, but the problem is that there's a grade there. When a grade is involved, it inevitably derails learning because what was intended to be a measure has now become the goal. If a student sees a grade they like, they'll sit back and relax. If they see a grade they don't like, maybe they will work harder to improve it, but they still aren't focused on learning.

Also, when looking at an online grade book, students are often bombarded by all sorts of information, not all of it relevant to what they are learning. If we want students to act on the data we give them, we must do what we can to target the information that is most relevant to the purpose at hand.

I don't want to say that the online grade book is useless, though. It's still possible to use the online grade book and built-in reporting features to help students focus on their growth and learning. One way to do this is to have students categorize their scores for assignments. I've found that it works best to do this at spaced intervals, typically before conferencing, so it's a bit more efficient than trying to do it every time you enter a new assignment. Even if you haven't switched your grade book to a standards-based approach, this will still work. You can identify specific assignments that focused on one skill and have students transfer those scores onto a separate document, maybe one that looks like Image 5.1.

Skill	Skill Description		
Assignment	Assignment #1 Name	Assignment #2 Name	Assignment #3 Name
Score	Score	Score	Score

Image 5.1: Assignment categorizing activity.

Even if we have a task-based online grade book, with a quick activity, students now have data they can use to focus on their learning. We've gotten rid of the grade element and sequenced the assessment data so students can reflect on growth.

No matter how you do it, the goal is for each student to get curated information focused only on what they are learning to help them make decisions about how and what to learn. Whatever that may look like, your goal in this step is to figure out a plan to make this happen. Maybe work with your district IT staff to determine how to get the online grade book to pull the type of report you want, perhaps develop a template students can use to record their data in more meaningful ways, or possibly play with tools that let you create custom mastery reports. You want your students to end up having usable data to inform their learning.

Develop your pre-conference reflection activities.

Consistency is key. While you may need to change some of the wording of these reflection activities depending on the content, the more you can keep consistent from conference to conference, the more comfortable students will be with the routine. Once students understand the routine and are comfortable with the prompts, they can focus on the learning itself. It also helps them practice so they get better at reflecting with similar prompts. The number you have depends on how you want to approach the different conferences. I have three of them—one for each type of conference.

For my mid-unit conferences, their reflection sheet asks them to share their strongest work so far from the unit (often a copy-and-pasted piece of writing) and explain what they are proud of in this work. The second piece has a series of questions and prompts that go as follows: (1) What are some concepts or ideas you're struggling with that we've been focusing on? (2) What do you think is the most important of those concepts? (3) Be specific. What are the smaller pieces of this concept that are giving you trouble? (4) Choose one or two of the most important small concepts and phrase them as a question you can ask me during the conference. This process helps them pin down precisely what we need to talk about. These reflection prompts usually take around fifteen minutes for students to do.

For my end-of-unit conferences, the reflection sheet begins with a prompt to have students go back to their learning portfolios and add what they've learned about each skill for the unit and then to make sure they have a strong example of their work that demonstrates their skills for each concept. The second prompt is general, and it asks them what they are proud of in terms of their growth and performance in this unit. This gives us a chance to talk about their wins. For the next prompt, while I have the learning progressions on the wall, I take them off my reflection sheet. The question asks, "How well would you say that you have learned each of the skills listed below? Explain your answer with specific things you've learned or are still stuck on." While I encourage students to use the progressions posted in the room as a support, I've found that when I had them on the page, students just copied down the levels they knew as their explanation. This piece helps us agree on an accurate score for each of the skills.

For my end-of-term conference, the reflection sheet zooms out and focuses on the big picture. I typically share a report with them with their scores for the term that we've already agreed upon in our end-of-unit conference. Then the first question is, "What do you want me to know about your learning and performance this term that the scores don't show?" This ends up being my favorite part of the discussion. It creates space for us to discuss that grades aren't everything, and students learn to advocate for themselves. The last part of this reflection sheet is forward-focused. I ask students, "Based on your performance and experience this term, what are two major goals you have for yourself and your learning next term?" To be honest, this step is difficult the first time around. Most students will just set a goal about getting better grades or trying to get an A. It takes a bit of talking through what good goals look like before you get a specific and helpful goal for the next term, but once students understand and feel like they control the goals they set for themselves, it's much more motivating than generic goals or ones set by someone else.

STEP 1   STEP 2   STEP 3   STEP 4   STEP 5

Develop follow-up activities.

While this isn't necessarily part of the conference itself, this step is crucial in turning those conversations into action. For this step, ask yourself, "What will students do with the information we discuss?" We can think about this in a couple of ways.

First, think about where students will record the information you discuss in your learning conference. I have done this in a few different ways, and I wouldn't say there's a right or wrong way to do it if the information is easily accessible to the student later. Currently, my approach is to have students record the notes from our conversation in their feedback portfolio, which we discussed in the previous chapter. However, I've also had students record this feedback in a dedicated space on their pre-conference reflection sheet or record it in their learning portfolios. I've even created a separate document exclusively to record notes from all the conferences during the year. However you do it, make sure students will look at it again later.

Second, think about how students could take the information from the conference and apply it to their learning. This might mean that at the end of your conference days, you provide an activity for students to practice the skills you discussed, possibly with them targeting specific skills or concepts you agreed upon as key focuses during the conference. It takes the information from being a concept they should think about to one with a sense of immediacy, which always helps students see the learning as important and boost motivation.

Another approach I've taken is to provide an independent learning opportunity after the conference. This ranges anywhere from a structured activity with guided resources to a completely open-ended activity with reflection questions as a guide. In addition, these can be short activities that take fifteen minutes, or they could be a multi-class process. For example, one of my favorite simple follow-up activities is to take the skills you're focusing on (I'll use four for this example) and put them on an interactive document so you can paste resources for students to explore. It might look similar to Image 5.2.

SKILL 1	SKILL 2	SKILL 3	SKILL 4
Video or Text Resource	Video or Text Resource	Video or Text Resource	Video or Text Resource

Image 5.2: Data reflection activity.

Then as a follow-up, I ask students to share out, first with a partner and then with the class, the most important nugget they learned from the resources. Not only does it help the student fill in the gaps in their understanding, but it also becomes a collaborative activity where students are learning from their peers, helping us have a productive discussion as a class.

As another approach, I sometimes take away the resources and add in an element where students provide evidence to show what they've learned. That document might look like Image 5.3.

WHAT SKILL DID YOU FOCUS ON?	
WHAT RESOURCES DID YOU USE TO LEARN MORE ABOUT THE SKILL?	
WHAT DID YOU LEARN ABOUT THE SKILL YOU WERE STUDYING? (EXPLAIN AS MUCH AS YOU CAN)	
PLEASE LINK OR ATTACH WHATEVER YOU USED TO DEMONSTRATE YOUR LEARNING.	

Image 5.3: Additional learning attempt.

The benefit of this method is that even if we just had an end-of-unit conference, it gives the students an additional attempt to show me what they know. At times, I will limit what they can do to demonstrate the skill. For example, I may tell students they will revise an old piece of writing to show how they've grown in the skill they focused on. At other times, I may leave it open-ended for students to demonstrate their learning however they think is best for them.

The important part isn't necessarily what they do. Rather, it's that they get a chance to take the discussion you had and turn it into action, to apply their learning, and to transform the discussion into growth. Without this, students will begin to see those conferences as just a box to check, but if they get a chance to immediately see increases in their performance as a result of the discussion, they will understand their value.

STEP 1   **STEP 2**   **STEP 3**   **STEP 4**   **STEP 5**

Test it out, reflect, test it out, reflect.

As you get ready to try it out, I recommend starting small. Focus on one skill in the conference the first time, or maybe one question you discuss in each conference. Don't wait until you feel like it's going to go perfectly, though. Just like anything else with teaching, no matter how long we spend planning, something will always throw a wrench in it. It's better to have a strong structure and then jump in and adapt as you go. Find an upcoming unit and develop a plan for how you can run these conferences with the unit.

Be intentional in your reflection, both independently and with your students. I have shared what works well for me, and I write this with the full knowledge that you will figure out what works best for you, your teaching style, and your kids.

Most importantly, have fun with it. This is a great chance to build relationships with students, talk about learning, and reach

each student wherever they're at. While the learning is important and the routines and resources must be in place, we can't lose sight of the fact that these conferences are a great opportunity to have the type of impact on students that many of us go into teaching to pursue.

OVERCOMING PUSHBACK

When I talk about student conferences, the pushback is never about the conferences. When teachers think about sitting down with a student one-on-one to help them uncover misconceptions, celebrate their growth, and set goals for themselves, no one pushes back against that. Where the pushback comes from is the context we are placed in when we teach inside a school system with crowded classrooms, rigid scheduling, and often unrealistic curriculum expectations. Here are the most common pieces of pushback I hear and how I respond to them.

I don't have time to do this with everything I have to cover in the curriculum. I first want to acknowledge the reality that it is difficult to do what you know is right when you are in an environment where you feel restricted in ensuring you cover the whole curriculum. As an encouragement to question that process, focus on the fact that covering a whole curriculum too quickly for students to learn is a pointless endeavor. As discussed earlier in the book, it's important to identify your priority standards and focus on those, ensuring students have full understanding. Prioritizing my instructional time around these high-leverage pieces of learning helps me be more efficient in my teaching, and when I do that, I notice that it frees up more of my time.

This process doesn't take as much time out of what we're already doing as it may sound like it will. My pre-conference activities usually take around fifteen minutes for the smaller conferences and thirty minutes for the larger conferences. Yes, that part does come out of instructional time. The conferences themselves, though, don't take time away from other activities because often, the conferences can happen during the same activities I would have done, and I might just have to tweak them a bit.

I had this same fear when I began incorporating student conferences, but it turns out that I hardly had to change anything I was teaching. Instead, I had to be more intentional about *how* I was teaching to free me up a bit more to work with students one-on-one.

What about the student who isn't motivated to participate in class? Learning conferences without any evidence of learning to talk about can get tricky, but they are still important for that student. For starters, we must realize an important truth about the students who refuse to attempt to engage in learning, which I've mentioned previously. Before we attempted to learn, we had the ability to tell ourselves that we could be successful. We have yet to prove differently to ourselves or others, but once we've attempted to learn a concept or skill or demonstrate that learning, we lose the ability to be hypothetical about our possibility for success. Once we've tried, we know the truth, but many students don't want to confront that truth because it means identifying shortcomings in their learning. For students who don't have a ton of academic confidence, this prospect is terrifying. As such, the act of not engaging can be the result of trying to preserve their ability to tell themselves they can do it.

With that perspective in mind, the student who doesn't engage and shuts down during times when they are given ownership over their learning is the student I meet with first. The benefit of providing ownership for students, thus removing the obligation of content delivery from yourself for this time, is that it frees you up to work one-on-one with students. During this time, I will go over and sit with the student. My goal isn't to walk them through the process; it's not to take on the responsibility for them. My goal is to help them find their first win. Sometimes that's all they need—just a quick win to tell them they've got this and can be successful. That's what I try to focus on during the learning conference, even if it's just me asking them a question and then celebrating when they can answer it in the moment. To be clear, this win needs to be grounded in real evidence of understanding at some level, not just fake praise that isn't founded on anything.

It might be the case that the student still doesn't want to engage even after that. This is tricky. It's one of those moments that demonstrates how much student motivation is a balancing act and how much it changes from student to student. The student might have a situation going on that they are trying to avoid, and they just need to put their head down. They might be frustrated because they tried and failed already, and they're not ready to try again. My goal in this moment is to listen to the student and to understand that, in this state, the student's brain isn't ready to learn. I have the benefit of teaching my ninth grade students all year long, so I know that I have time with this student. They may not be ready to learn it today, but they might be ready tomorrow.

Do I want to enable this kind of behavior? Absolutely not, but I've also found that trying to lay down the law in this moment won't result in productive work in the future. My approach with this student is to say something like, "I care about you. Something seems to be going on. If I let you have time to process it today, can I count on you to learn this when you're ready?" This approach—demonstrating care, naming the current reality, and offering a mutually beneficial solution—often goes a long way. I've seen students pop up to begin working after I've walked away. I've seen students come back the next day and thank me for understanding before working extra hard that class period to catch up.

Let's be honest about this scenario, though. The student likely wasn't going to engage that day, regardless of the instructional approach used. Incorporating ownership allowed me to have the space and flexibility to hold that conversation with the student. In other instructional approaches where I might be more tied down to a group or direct instruction, I probably wouldn't have the time for that conversation. Ownership may not have caused the problem, but it created the space for me to try to solve it.

My students aren't productive when I'm not in the room monitoring them. My response to this: I teach ninth grade. I totally get this point and feel it really strongly, especially at the beginning of the year. This is why the first recommendation in the section about what you can do tomorrow is to practice building stamina with independent work. Students, frankly, are rarely asked to monotask. Their lives are full of cognitive switches as they bounce from watching a show to talking to friends to scrolling social media, and that's just a three-second snapshot of their day. Students (and us) live in a world that doesn't value extended periods of focus. We can be more mindful of this and (1) have grace as we begin this process and (2) accept that it is our responsibility to help build their capacity to focus if we want everyone involved to reap the benefits of it.

I have another response to this pushback, and this one will make some people nervous. It's a confession. When I am in learning conferences with my students, the rest of the room typically is less productive than it is when I'm in there. I've been doing learning conferences for years, and it's still this way. It's a fact I've come to accept because after so many times doing it, the benefit of those one-on-one conversations with students far outweighs the benefit of having more focus for a couple of days of instruction and practice. It's a tradeoff. I could stay in the room and monitor the class to get slightly more productivity from the whole group, or I could focus my energy on helping individual students reflect on their learning and set goals for themselves. The latter has longer-lasting impacts, in my experience, because when we return from conferences, students often have a boost in motivation to pursue their learning goals.

You may come up with a solution to this issue. You can hold the learning conferences from inside the room so you can monitor students and help keep them on track. I tend to not do this because I am constantly distracted. A few things can help, and they are no different than what I do when I'm in the room. First, use a timer. Also, display on the board how many people have finished an assignment. I use Google Classroom, and at the time of this writing, all I have to do is go to the classwork pages and click on the assignment. Once I've done that, it will anonymously show how many people are done versus how many aren't. That little bit of added positive peer pressure can be helpful.

Again, while many little tricks can help, I don't want to send the message that your goal should be to achieve complete focus in the classroom. Your goal is to have the most productive and supportive conversation you can with the student who's in front of you, and then your secondary aim is to help ensure students are still productive in the room. If those priorities get switched during the conferences, it will diminish the value of this process because it's hard to be present in the moment when our priorities are elsewhere.

THE HACK IN ACTION
BY NICHOLAS EMMANUELE, HIGH SCHOOL ELA TEACHER
AND DEPARTMENT CHAIR, ERIE, PENNSYLVANIA

The following is an introduction and a Q&A regarding assessment practices and learning conferences.

I teach English Language Arts in a suburban school district under an intensified block (semester) schedule, with classes every day for eighty minutes for half of the year. While I teach one section of ninth grade Honors English each year, I predominantly co-teach Academic (College Preparation) English Language Arts with my special education co-teacher, where we loop from ninth grade to tenth grade with our classes. We've been co-teaching together since the 2011–2012 school year.

What problem were you facing? I had been wrestling with assessment practices for years because I did not feel my traditional practices were capturing what students knew or could do. Students did not have ownership of their learning. I first worked on cutting back on grading homework, then my co-teacher and I shifted to some gamification to track practice as XP ("experience points"), and finally, we shifted to letter grades only instead of random points and to aligning all practice to standards (or learning targets). This led us to evaluating what students could do in relation to our standards, but we did not feel our evaluations were enough. Students were writing more, taking up independent reading, and exploring vocabulary with a new digital program the district purchased. We wanted to give students more say in assessments. I knew we needed to shift to a workshop model where students could talk about their learning and receive more meaningful feedback and action steps. In the end, our goal was for students to "pitch" to us the grade their evidence aligned with.

How did you implement a strategy to give students ownership of their learning? Conferencing began to take center stage in our classroom (as well as in my Honors English sections, where our gifted support teacher would co-teach a couple times a week with me). We structured our classroom so students had time to read each day, we touched base as a class with Smiles and Frowns (inspired by Washington State educator Monte Syrie), we'd teach for fifteen to twenty minutes, and then students had time to explore, work, watch instructional videos that reiterated our full-group lessons, and learn. During this last segment of class, we began conferring with students. This allowed for individualization, but then we realized we needed to begin teaching students how to reflect if we were going to ask them to take ownership and pitch their grades. Our process included the following:

- **In-Class Conferring:** While it is not usually possible to confer with each student every day, some students may only require one or two minutes of check-in while others may benefit from five or more minutes. Conferring with any student (or small group of students) can include reiterating directions, helping them get started, talking through misconceptions, listening to their thought processes, or pushing thinking (or reading or writing) forward. These conversations allow us to provide in-process, formative feedback that students can directly apply to their thinking, reading, writing, or tasks at hand. This limits the amount of written feedback we leave. It also provides us space to gauge student learning progress before they even submit work.

- **Weekly Reflections:** We scaffold weekly reflections based on that week's learning target(s). At first, we provide sentence stems that ask definitions of new terms, examples from the week's work, or reflections/thoughts/feelings on progress. These eventually turn into keywords for students to develop a reflection, and then eventually, students are only given the language of the learning target(s). This requires modeling. When we first implemented grade pitches, students didn't know what to do, and we had not prepared them for in-depth thinking on their progress. Weekly check-ins (especially because we're on a semester schedule) allow for practice before the five-week grade pitch.

▶ **Grade Pitches:** With continual conferring and weekly written reflections (and my usual review of their work, a standards-based approach that utilizes 0s, 1s, 2s, or 3s in the grade book that do not average together), students eventually reach a five-week grade pitch. The mid-quarter pitch is replaced by the quarter grade pitch. Students are given at least one class period (usually a bit more than one) to complete the grade pitch reflection, which prompts them to include evidence of their learning for the relevant course-level learning targets (of which there are six). These course-level targets are broader than the specific weekly learning target(s), but evidence of the weekly targets is used to compare the proficiency of the course-level targets. In the end, we discuss together and determine a grade based on their evidence and what we have been seeing as teachers.

What was the outcome of the new strategy you used? Students have been able to talk more confidently about what they are learning and can do in English Language Arts class now. They are not reciting a percentage of their averaged points, but they can identify specific sentences they wrote, discuss the novels they have read, and detail their work. This ownership of their learning has shown students that they can be successful readers, writers, speakers, and thinkers.

Learning conferences have made such a significant impact on the culture of learning and the dynamic of my classroom. I feel it in the little moments, like when I walk up to a student and ask them what they are focusing on in their learning. I used to get canned responses that named some sort of general principle we're working on, but now I frequently hear students cite a specific detail about a concept they're stuck on. I feel it in the moments when I can walk up to a student and say, "Remember when we talked about X for you to focus on? I see you just did it correctly there." I hear it in the moments when students are in peer reflection groups and have to ask for feedback, and instead of everyone listing the same responses they think they're supposed to say, I hear each student say a specific detail they know their peer needs to focus on. I see it in the moments when a student sits down with me for a conference, and I can get a smile out of them by pointing out the areas where I've seen them grow.

I don't want to paint the picture that it's always sunshine and rainbows when it comes to student conferences. There are still times when I have a round of conferences and then walk away thinking, "How did that feel so pointless?" It's tough. Not every conversation will result in leaps and bounds in each student's learning. It's a three-, four-, or five-minute conversation. Learning is too complex to be solved in that amount of time.

What I will say, though, is that learning feels much more personal as a result of these conferences, and when we care personally about what we're doing, it's much easier to tap into our motivation. The process of sitting down with each student to talk with them feels like it humanizes a process that often feels dehumanizing to many students. Nobody is motivated in an environment where they feel like they don't really matter or that they are just another face in the crowd. It helps me get to know them better, and it helps students truly know that I am on their side and care about their learning. When students know that I am invested in them as individuals, when they can see the specific ways they can improve, and when they trust that I am on their side, it makes a world of difference in student learning.

Think about the last student who came in for help outside of class time, especially one who you haven't quite clicked with yet or who was only in there because they were forcing themselves to work on an assignment. When they walked away from your classroom, what changed? For me, I usually have a better understanding of that student, and that means I know more about how to teach them. I usually have built trust and a stronger relationship with the student. When a student and a teacher trust each other, it creates a better environment for learning to take place.

CONCLUSION

Bring Your Dream Classroom to Life

As we draw to the end of the book, take a second to take what might be the most important action you can as you prepare for the next steps in your journey. In a second, I want you to close your eyes and imagine your classroom where assessment is being used intentionally. What does it look like when students are motivated and excited to learn? What does it look like when students build their confidence by celebrating their competence? What does it look like when they're taking ownership of their learning using learning progressions?

Now take a second and envision that. I really mean it. Close your eyes and paint that picture. You can include some of the most memorable students you've had, and place that image directly in your own classroom. I know it may sound ridiculous, but before you get to the next paragraph, imagine your dream classroom.

Okay, thank you for doing the exercise. Another step is to write a description of that classroom and put it where you'll see it regularly. I have one posted on the wall behind my desk, and I update it every year. I put it there for two reasons. The first is for my students. I want them to know that I'm growing, learning, and setting goals for myself to model how I want them to be.

However, the more important reason I have it there is that sometimes I need it. At times, this feels like it's going off the rails. You might try something, and it blows up in your face. Early in my process, students got so confused by a new process I tried that it just completely fell apart. As I adjusted, I occasionally made changes that buried me in work. In those moments, I wanted to quit. I wanted to stop putting in energy to make changes because I felt like they just didn't matter.

In those moments, the only motivator for me was a powerful vision of why what I was doing mattered. That vision always centered on my students. When we talk about assessment, it's easy to get wrapped up in the pedagogy and the practice, but none of that is really why we do it. Why we do it is that we believe there is a better way for classrooms to function, and we know that we work with young people who deserve the best we have to offer. When we approach our assessment practices through the lens of building motivation in our students, it dramatically changes how we think about it and implement it in our classroom.

As we wrap up *Hacking Student Motivation*, I have three final messages to convey, and the first is this: **You don't have to do this alone.** I started all this assessment work with a closed door. I did everything, found all the resources, tried and failed over and over, and didn't find anyone to be a buddy through that process. If I could do it all over again, my priority would be to find someone else who wants to work on assessment practices that build student motivation. You could even organize a cohort of teachers to do this work together. Not only is it infinitely more enjoyable, but it also can lessen the burden you have to carry. I really am asking you to find people who you can connect with on this topic. These might be colleagues in your school, a friend in another district, or an online community of teachers who are passionate about the same ideas (more of us are out there than you expect).

The second message I want to share goes along with the last one. **Don't push yourself to do everything all at once.** This is a long process. You can make plenty of small changes that will lead to huge shifts, and those changes don't all need to happen at once. Give yourself grace. One of the hardest parts for me in my assessment journey is that once my eyes had been opened to a better way, I often felt like I was doing my students a disservice previously, and I rushed as quickly as I could into a different approach. I've learned that I can't fix everything now, but I can fix one thing at a time. As you do that, recognize that your willingness to grow and change is one of the most important gifts you can give to your students, and once they recognize that willingness in you, they are some of the most understanding people in the world. They will see your intentions, they will notice the small changes, and they will be grateful. Countless times in my career, my students were the ones who reminded me of the importance of growth when I found myself frustrated that I hadn't reached the end of the growing, and through this, I got to model for them what it looks like to be motivated to learn something, even when it's hard.

The last message, and the most important one, is two simple words that I can absolutely guarantee you don't hear enough: **thank you.**

I don't mean that as a thank you for purchasing and reading this book (although I am incredibly grateful for that, too). What I mean is thank you for doing one of the most difficult jobs in the world. Every day, you invest so much of yourself into a job that, though it may not always feel this way, truly has the power to change the world. Every day, you must try to be the force that rights the inequities in our world in small but oh-so-important ways within your classroom. Every day, you give students the best possible experience by caring about them, about your practice, and about our future. On top of all that, here you are, trying to grow and improve your practice because you believe we can make learning and life better for the kids we serve.

If you've seen me present, you've probably seen me tear up when I say this. Honestly, it's not a real Tyler Rablin workshop unless I've teared up during the course of it. As embarrassing as it is (not because it happens but because I'm writing this in a public place), I want you to know that I have tears in my eyes as I write this. You deserve to feel so proud of what you've done, what you do every day, and what you will do for kids in the future. It is truly one of the biggest honors of my life to be a part of this profession because of the people I share that honor with—all of you.

So, here we are at the end, which is still far from an ending. It's a beginning for some and a continuation for others. Remember, the goal isn't to find the end of the journey; it's to find the next steps … and then the next and then the next. I know what my next steps are in my journey, and I hope this book helped you find your next steps, gave you the confidence to take those steps, and empowered you to believe that you can truly continue to make a difference through it all because when it comes down to it, helping students tap into their motivation, find their confidence in their abilities to learn, and feel successful in what they do in the classroom are part of the noblest journeys we can embark on as educators.

REFERENCES

Jonsson, Anders, and Gunilla Svingby. "The Use of Scoring Rubrics: Reliability, Validity and Educational Consequences." *Educational Research Review* 2, no. 2 (2007): 130–44. https://doi.org/10.1016/j.edurev.2007.05.002.

Kluger, Avraham N., and Angelo DeNisi. "The Effects of Feedback Interventions on Performance: A Historical Review, a Meta-Analysis, and a Preliminary Feedback Intervention Theory." *Psychological Bulletin* 119, no. 2 (1996): 254–84. https://doi.org/10.1037/0033-2909.119.2.254.

Nicol, David J., and Debra Macfarlane-Dick. "Formative Assessment and Self-regulated Learning: A Model and Seven Principles of Good Feedback Practice." *Studies in Higher Education* 31, no. 2 (January 24, 2007): 199–218. https://doi.org/10.1080/03075070600572090.

Quinn, David M. "Experimental Evidence on Teachers' Racial Bias in Student Evaluation: The Role of Grading Scales." *Educational Evaluation and Policy Analysis* 42, no. 3 (June 22, 2020): 375–92. https://doi.org/10.3102/0162373720932188.

Von Bergen, Clarence, Martin Bressler, and Kitty Campbell. "The Sandwich Feedback Method: Not Very Tasty." *Journal of Behavioral Studies in Business* 7 (September 2014).

ABOUT THE AUTHOR

Tyler Rablin is an instructional technology coach and former high school language arts teacher for Sunnyside School District in Sunnyside, Washington. His passion for education centers on how intentional technology integration, modernized assessment practices, and strong cultures of learning can provide meaningful, powerful, and personal learning experiences for each student.

In addition to his work in Sunnyside, he works with other schools through Tyler Rablin Consulting to support assessment practices and technology integration in the classroom. In his free time, he enjoys wildlife photography, reading sci-fi and fantasy, and hiking with his wife and two dogs. Connect with Tyler Rablin at tylerrablin.com or on X at @Mr_Rablin.

ACKNOWLEDGMENTS

This book wouldn't have happened without the support and inspiration of so many people, and while it seems impossible to capture my gratitude for all of them, I'll give it my best shot.

First and foremost, I would like to thank my wife, MaryBeth, for supporting me as I ran off alone to the mountains for weeks at a time to write in our little camper. You were my encouragement when I would get stumped and my sounding board when I needed the opinion of someone I trust and respect immensely. I am inspired daily by the work you do in your own classroom. I love you.

Bonus shout-out to my dogs, Sunny and Shadow, for all the snuggles and hikes when I needed some stress relief during this process.

Next, thank you to my friends and family for making me even more excited about the process. To everyone who celebrated with me as I finished each step in the process, listened as I explained a concept in the book I was struggling to express clearly, or simply asked me how things were going with the book, you all gave me the boost I needed.

While some of my friends will also fall into this category, thank you to my colleagues for inspiring me and pushing me to be better. This goes all the way back to my years at Mac-Hi in Milton-Freewater, Oregon. I wouldn't have made it through those early years without the support of my colleagues, but I would be remiss not to specifically mention my first principal, Ralph. He was the leader I needed early in my career to help me get my priorities set right. He taught me what it means to truly care about the young people we get the opportunity to work with, to recognize that our role means caring about the community instead of just the school, and that the rules of school are always meant to be broken when they aren't working for the kids or their learning.

To my colleagues and leaders in Sunnyside, thank you. We went through some of the most stressful times education has seen in a while, and many of you gave me the encouragement I needed on the days I was struggling, whether that was just a smile in the hallway or a deep talk over a beer. I feel so fortunate to work in a district that takes care of its people (even when those people ask to go off on a limb and do something way outside the box).

A big thank you to Jason Aguilar, Kelly Castle, Vanessa Ellis, Nicholas Emmanuele, Toni Stephens, and Angela Stockman for helping me paint a picture of what these Hacks really look like in the classroom and bringing their own twists to the concept to show that these ideas aren't designed to be followed like a script but to be remixed in each individual classroom to meet the unique needs there.

Finally, a big shout-out to the Times10 Publications team for the opportunity to write this book and for their support along the way.

HACK
6

GENERATE FEEDBACK LOOPS
Analyze, Revise, and Improve

Grading does not improve learning, in the same way
a scale does not cause someone to lose weight.
— TOM SCHIMMER, AUTHOR AND SPEAKER

THE PROBLEM: Grades are terrible feedback

WE'VE WATCHED THIS scene unfold in our classrooms: students receive a graded assignment with the teacher's marks in the column, noting errors or commendations. Students flip past these comments to the back page. When the student finds the score, they shove the assignment into their backpack. Or dump it into the trash can. They received the grade, so the learning stops; there is nothing else for them to do.

Grades present so many problems, including:

- Grades are outcomes.

- Grades stall progress.

- Grades prevent risk-taking.

- Grades provide no opportunity for improvement.

- Grades are one-way streets.

- Grades are not tools for learning.

In high school, when athletes don't perform well in an event, they often badger the coach for help. Athletes' reactions are intuitive—when faced with a problem, they look for feedback with the intent to incorporate it. What can they eat to make them stronger? What can they do to build endurance? How can they improve their stroke? When can they schedule extra laps? The problem is that students rarely seek out or implement this kind of feedback in the classroom.

We want students to receive and to give feedback. Students need to know what is working and what isn't, and feedback helps students identify behaviors to continue or modify.

THE HACK: Generate feedback loops

Generating feedback loops is an essential part of process-based assessment, just like encouraging practice instead of perfection, relinquishing control, producing positive competition, and developing the inner voice. Instead of assessing through grades or criticism, assess through feedback. It is best when given in real time, either verbally or in writing. If it must be shared later, consider recording observations using voice apps or videos so students can hear the tone.

Feedback sources can include:

- formal or informal teacher input on activities, papers, presentations, assignments, tests, homework, projects, and discussions

- students' input to each other

- students' self-assessments

- input from mentors, parents, or outside sources such as competitions, publications, or the public

Effective feedback:

- is evaluative rather than judgmental

- makes students feel better, not bitter

- can be taken seriously, not personally

- stimulates dialogue, discussion, or follow-up

- helps students understand how close they are to the goal

- helps students understand what they need to do to meet the goal

- inspires learning and modification

- illuminates areas of strength and areas to improve

- puts students in control of assessing themselves, their work, and their process

Consider using experiences from your life to emphasize feedback's usefulness. For example, my dad showed my mom a project he was working on—a cheese board with wooden pieces, where the colors created an optical illusion. Except, he flubbed the pattern and couldn't figure out how to fix it. My mom recognized his design from a quilt pattern. She helped him sort the colors into the right order. And it was a good thing: he was almost ready to glue it together with a slew of errors.

Although my mom is a retired choir teacher, she dabbles in writing. She drafts pieces and then brings them to me for feedback. We talk about her writing, and I point out where I'm confused; I ask her questions, and I give suggestions. My mom takes these same pieces to a writing group that includes a cohort of writers from young professionals to retirees like herself. She works through several rounds of advice and drafts before submitting the work to journals. She knows there are no right or wrong suggestions, and she appreciates receiving contradicting opinions. She's gathering responses to her work, developing her skills, and making updates.

We want students to do the same and frame feedback as neutral. Help students view setbacks as opportunities for growth. The goal is for students to make their processes more successful, to engage with reactions in order to improve, and to create and practice sustainable habits. Each student is at a different place and will benefit differently from feedback. Being a successful practitioner is about nuance. Feedback should follow suit and be multilayered, diverse, and incremental. Think of feedback as the way you differentiate and personalize your instruction and assessment.

Feedback can encourage students to continue on the same path or to change direction. You want to help students understand that they can make a change instead of making an excuse. The best feedback:

- uses specific details (avoid "nice" or "good job" or "wow")

- helps students understand why something works or doesn't

- suggests research methods

- makes connections from the student's work to something else

- asks questions that encourage reflection

According to Douglas Stone and Sheila Heen, authors of *Thanks for the Feedback*, there are three types of feedback: gratitude, coaching, and evaluation. Use each of these for different situations. Sometimes students need to know their effort or performance is recognized (gratitude); sometimes they need assistance (coaching); and at other times, they need to know where they stand against the goal (evaluation).

As students practice habits and develop skills, allow for multiple approaches and be timely and specific with your feedback. Afford students the chance to think about changes, and offer confirmation when they move in a constructive direction.

Before students perform, provide opportunities to receive input from a variety of sources. A few weeks before the state music competition, a choir director hired a respected music educator to serve as a clinician. The clinician listened to each madrigal, barbershop, and soloist. After the performances, the clinician provided assessments, including demonstrations of skills. The clinician helped students recognize areas that needed improvement (intonation, rhythmic accuracy, and tone quality) and processes that could assist (imagining the pitch, thinking high, listening, clapping rhythms, and blending).

EACH DAY REQUIRES A DIFFERENT EFFORT FROM YOU AND YOUR STUDENTS. CONTINUALLY IDENTIFY WHAT IS WORKING AND WHAT ISN'T.

Students used the clinician's feedback in the weeks leading up to the competition to improve their execution. Because students performed and received feedback in a group setting, others also identified common setbacks and areas of strength. Students said they appreciated learning new techniques (like tongue-twisters and warm-up chants) and hearing what their classmates executed successfully (diction, engaging an audience, and facial expressions). They also valued a professional's feedback prior to the state event.

Examine how you can give observations that will help students recognize their habits and processes, see how their determination affected their performance, and realize how their effort mattered. You may consider bringing in others, like a clinician, or allowing students to give feedback to each other. Students may also give themselves feedback that will help analyze how their habits and processes were fruitful. When students critique themselves, guide them to map out their processes in order to recognize that success is the result of controllable habits.

Examine the amount of information students receive. Too much is overwhelming. When students see only a few comments they need to address, they feel like the feedback is manageable. They may say to themselves:

- I know what I can do to make this section better.

- This is my best work.

- I'm on the right track.

As the teacher, focus on complimenting effort instead of achievement. Consider:

- "It looks like you're trying to use [specific skill] here. Can you use [that same skill] in other places?"

- "I see you implemented [a technique]. Where else can [this technique] be useful?"

- "You've worked hard on [a specific process]. This allows me to [specific effect]."

After students receive feedback, provide in-class time for them to make changes. You might consider assessing how or if students applied the feedback they've received. Examine your delivery medium. Do your students respond better to verbal feedback? Are they ready to handle it in a whole-class setting? Do they respond better to peers or themselves?

Finally, review your audience and the timing of your feedback. Throughout the year or semester, students' needs change. To generate awareness of and create movement in student work, circle back to nuance. Each day requires a different effort from you and your students. Continually identify what is working and what isn't. Be attuned to your students' needs. Observe conversations, body language, facial expressions, and emotions. You can skim a random sampling of student work, poll students (in-person using thumbs-up, neutral, or sideways or electronically through an app), or collect exit slips.

If you know a student is dealing with a breakup or grieving a grandparent, tread delicately with constructive feedback. Honor students' efforts, especially in trying times. Recognize their resolve and resilience and remember how students deal with feedback: personally. Then, help students accept it as a data point and not as a critique of themselves.

One of my students said:

> "One of the most helpful things about this class was your feedback. You always told me exactly what I did wrong on my pieces and gave me enough feedback to allow me to fix my mistakes and learn from them. However, it's not like you just flat out edited my piece and changed it yourself. I felt like you never just gave me what I was supposed to change, you would instead suggest a different direction. This is perfect for my learning because I feel like some teachers don't give you enough information to learn from your mistakes and just expect you to somehow know what you did wrong."

WHAT YOU CAN DO TOMORROW

Although teachers are accustomed to assessing at the end of a unit or project, it's more effective to provide immediate and daily feedback. Feedback can be informal or formal and is most effective when it gives students the opportunity to find their own mistakes, make purposeful choices, improve, and modify their processes to meet their goals.

- **Shift your mindset from grader to coach.** Gwen Jorgensen, as a high school senior, wanted to work on her stroke mechanics. During practices, her coach recorded an underwater video. After, he showed it to her, pointing out places where she could try different techniques. The purpose was to gather feedback on her performance well before the state meet. What was she doing right? What did she need to work on?

  A coach watches athletes at practice and studies film post-games to improve the team's performance. Coach—instead of grade—your students, and they will begin to see you as their biggest cheerleader and supporter. Build community, a team mentality, and inspire collaboration. Frequently check in. Help students see you advocate for their success. Allow them to practice and scaffold experiences. Work with your students and allow them to work together. Provide class time for students to give each other feedback, which helps create a teamwork mentality.

- **Model the process.** Students often struggle to give and receive effective and constructive feedback. Many students won't want to hurt someone's feelings, or they genuinely don't know what to say. Show students diplomatic tactics.

  Sometimes, I ask a student to work with me on a piece of writing in front of the class. I project a sample of my work and read it out loud. Then, I ask for the editor's reaction. When the student gives me feedback, I present follow-up questions and engage in a dialogue. I rephrase the feedback I'm given, such as: "What I hear you saying is ..." and "Am I understanding you correctly?". This allows the class to see me working through receiving, paraphrasing, and accepting feedback in a neutral way.

After modeling a feedback loop in front of the class, I ask students to journal on what they noticed about the process. As a class, we discuss what each student would have said and how they thought the loop could have improved. After this discussion, I share my plan to work with the feedback I received. I also present questions I want to ask my editor.

You might also share stories from your personal life. For example, my dad makes pallet clocks for family and friends. At each step in his process, he asks for feedback from the recipient. The first choice is about the wood: dark or light? Thick or thin? Rustic or refined? He offers a suggestion and then listens to the recipient's preferences. Once wooden slats are assembled and cut into a forty-four-inch circle, it's time for the numbers. Roman numerals or Arabic? Large or small? Black or white? Again, he offers his vision but decides based on feedback. Finally, he either leaves the wood natural or applies a finish that could be glossy or matte. My dad's goal is to make a clock that is accurate and visually appealing. He understands not everyone has the same aesthetic, and his goal is not just to produce a product but to hone his skills in both woodworking and listening to his customer. (See Image 6.1 to see various pallet clock options.) A feedback loop is crucial for his success.

Image 6.1

- **Practice soft skills.** Learning requires engaging with feedback to make constructive changes. Identify what's holding students back and build soft skills to help them move forward. Here are ideas you might consider for mini-lessons:
  - ‣ working collaboratively
  - ‣ managing time
  - ‣ making and implementing plans
  - ‣ meeting deadlines
  - ‣ thinking creatively
  - ‣ persevering
  - ‣ asking questions
  - ‣ resolving conflicts
  - ‣ advocating
  - ‣ listening

What activities would help your students practice soft skills? At my high school, students in a special education program run a café. During the Thanksgiving season, they make and sell pies. Orders are placed and fulfilled the week of Thanksgiving. Students learn to work together, manage orders, meet deadlines, and be creative with marketing. Students also receive responses from customers. Which pies were most popular? What can the students do to improve and expedite next year's process?

Buy *Hacking Student Learning Habits*
AVAILABLE AT:
Amazon.com
10Publications.com
and bookstores near you

MORE FROM
TIMES 10 PUBLICATIONS

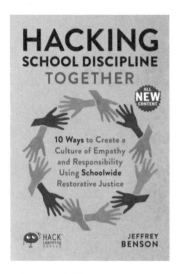

Hacking School Discipline Together

10 Ways to Create a Culture of Empathy and Responsibility Using Schoolwide Restorative Justice

By Jeffrey Benson

Hacking School Discipline Together is the sequel to *Hacking School Discipline*. This book, with all new content, goes beyond the classroom level and helps all administrators, teachers, and staff members create a culture of responsible students at the schoolwide and systemwide levels. Veteran educator Jeffrey Benson provides a road map to reduce stress around discipline and create staff unity, compassion, and consistency.

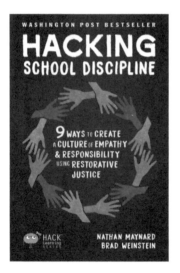

Hacking School Discipline

9 Ways to Create a Culture of Empathy & Responsibility Using Restorative Justice

By Nathan Maynard and Brad Weinstein

Reviewers proclaimed this original *Hacking School Discipline* book and *Washington Post* bestseller to be "maybe the most important book a teacher can read, a must for all educators, fabulous, a game-changer!" Teachers and presenters Maynard and Weinstein demonstrate how to eliminate punishment and build a culture of responsible students and independent learners at the classroom level. Twenty-one straight months at #1 on Amazon, *Hacking School Discipline* disrupted education in a big way.

Browse all titles at 10Publications.com

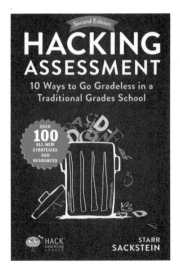

Hacking Assessment 2E
10 Ways to Go Gradeless In a Traditional Grades School
Starr Sackstein

Starr Sackstein is back with an updated road map for educators to hack grading and assessment. Readers will learn about the flaws of traditional assessment systems and how to make immediate changes so students can better advocate for themselves as learners. Begin by addressing your mindset about grading, and learn how to help your community buy into the shift to go gradeless. Bravely change the systems that aren't serving your students.

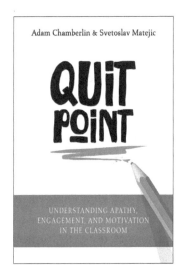

Quit Point
Understanding Apathy, Engagement, and Motivation in the Classroom
By Adam Chamberlin and Svetoslav Matejic

Authors Chamberlin and Matejic present a new way of approaching the Quit Point—how, why, and when students quit and how to stop quitting before it happens. Their insights will transform how teachers reach the potential of every student. *Quit Point* reveals how to confront apathy and build student engagement; differentiate learning for all levels; find interventions to challenge students to keep going; and use applications and tools to engage students starting tomorrow.

Browse all titles at 10Publications.com

Hacking the Writing Workshop
Redesign with Making in Mind
By Angela Stockman

Agility matters. This is what Angela Stockman learned when she left the classroom over a decade ago to begin supporting young writers and their teachers in schools. What she learned transformed her practice and led to the publication of her primer on this topic, *Make Writing*. Angela is back with more stories from the road and plenty of new thinking to share.

Even More Hacking Engagement
50 New Ways to Make Learning Fun for All Students
By James Alan Sturtevant

Boost your student engagement! If you and your students aren't approaching your class each day with excitement for the new ideas and learning surprises you're about to experience, then it's time to hack your student engagement. James Sturtevant wrote *Hacking Engagement* and *Hacking Engagement Again,* and now he's back with 50 new ways to make the classroom fun for everyone. Learn how to use tech to show pizzazz, improve your presentation skills, add anticipation and intrigue to each day, and inspire kids to higher-level thinking.

Browse all titles at 10Publications.com

RESOURCES FROM
TIMES 10 PUBLICATIONS

10Publications.com

Connect with us on social media:

@10Publications
@HackMyLearning
Times 10 Publications on Facebook
Times 10 Publications on LinkedIn

TIMES 10 PUBLICATIONS provides practical solutions that busy educators can read today and use tomorrow. We bring you content from experienced teachers and leaders, and we share it through books, podcasts, webinars, articles, events, and ongoing conversations on social media. Our books and materials help turn practice into action. Stay in touch with us at 10Publications.com and follow our updates on X @10Publications and #Times10News.

Made in United States
Troutdale, OR
06/01/2024

20252747R00120